THE POWER OF STUBBORNNESS

BY **MAYUR SOMANI**

notionpress.com

INDIA · SINGAPORE · MALAYSIA

ISBN
Hardcase 979-8-89744-610-0
Paperback 979-8-89724-556-7

They told you to stop being stubborn. They said it was a flaw—a weakness.

But what if they were wrong?

Some of the greatest minds, innovators, and survivors in history succeeded not because they gave up, but because they refused to.

This book isn't about changing who you are—it's about helping you discover how to use your stubbornness as your greatest strength.

If you've ever been doubted, rejected, or told you couldn't do something, this is your guide to proving them all wrong.

Ready to turns your stubbornness into success? Let's begin.

Contents

CHAPTER 1

The Misunderstood Strength

Introduction: The Hidden Power of Stubbornness

From childhood, we are taught that **stubbornness is a flaw.**

Parents scold their children for refusing to listen. Teachers reward obedience over defiance. Workplaces promote those who comply with company culture rather than those who challenge it. Society, as a whole, values **conformity over resistance.**

The message is clear:

- ✓ **Obedience is good.**
- ✓ **Defiance is bad.**
- ✓ **Compromise leads to success.**

But history tells a different story.

Some of the **greatest innovators, revolutionaries, and leaders were also the most stubborn individuals.** Their refusal to quit, their ability to hold their vision steady despite opposition, and their resilience in the face of failure set them apart.

- **Thomas Edison ignored failure.** After more than 1,000 failed attempts to create the lightbulb, he famously said, *"I have not failed. I've just found 1,000 ways that won't work."*
- **Michael Jordan refused to accept rejection.** After being cut from his high school basketball team, he didn't quit—he

practiced harder, trained longer, and became one of the greatest athletes in history.

- **Serena Williams defied expectations.** Critics said she would never dominate women's tennis. She **proved them wrong—again and again—becoming one of the most decorated athletes of all time.**

None of these individuals succeeded **despite** their stubbornness.

They succeeded **because of it.**

So, if stubbornness is a trait that fuels success, why does society teach us to suppress it?

In this chapter, we'll **redefine stubbornness, uncover why it's discouraged, and explore how to harness it as a powerful tool for success.**

Phase 1: Why Society Teaches Us to Suppress Stubbornness

Stubbornness is misunderstood—not because it lacks value, but because it disrupts **order, predictability, and control.**

From childhood to adulthood, we are conditioned to believe that **obedience leads to success,** while defiance leads to trouble. This happens in three key stages:

1. Early Childhood: Stubbornness vs. Obedience

👶 Imagine a toddler refusing to eat vegetables, insisting on wearing mismatched clothes, or throwing a tantrum at bedtime. How do parents typically respond?

- *"Stop being so stubborn!"*
- *"Why can't you just listen?"*
- *"Do as you're told!"*

At this stage, **stubbornness is labeled as disobedience.**

But what if we reframed it?

💡 **A child's stubbornness is an early display of individuality, curiosity, and decision-making.**

- When a child **insists on doing something their own way,** they're developing independence.
- When they **refuse to accept "because I said so" as an answer,** they're practicing critical thinking.
- When they **persist despite opposition,** they're building resilience.

Instead of suppressing stubbornness, what if parents **taught children to direct it productively?**

◆ **Example:** Instead of saying, *"Stop being stubborn!"* a parent could say,

☞ *"I love that you have strong opinions. Let's talk about why this matters to you."*

By shifting the conversation, the child learns that **being strong-willed isn't bad—it's a skill.**

2. The School System: Compliance Over Questioning

📊 As children enter school, the conditioning continues. Schools prioritize **order, structure, and uniformity** over independent thought.

- ✓ **Follow instructions without questioning them.**
- ✓ **Raise your hand before speaking.**
- ✓ **Memorize, don't challenge.**
- ✓ **Stick to standardized answers.**

For children who naturally **question authority,** this environment can feel suffocating. Instead of fostering curiosity, schools often correct what they see as **"disruptive behavior."**

◈ How Schools Suppress Stubbornness

- **Challenging a teacher's perspective is labeled as disrespectful.**
- **Thinking outside the box is often dismissed in favor of "correct" methods.**
- **Persistence in debating an idea is seen as being difficult rather than determined.**

💡 **Real education should cultivate stubbornness—not suppress it.**

Imagine if:

- **Galileo had accepted what his teachers told him** about the Earth being the center of the universe.
- **Marie Curie had believed that women shouldn't study science.**
- **Albert Einstein had stopped questioning authority** when he was labeled a "poor student."

History is made by **those who choose defiance over compliance.**

3. The Workplace: Adaptability is Rewarded, Defiance is Punished

🔨 As we enter adulthood, the expectation to conform **doesn't disappear—it intensifies.**

Workplaces **claim** to value innovation, leadership, and creativity. But in reality:

- ✓ Employees who comply with company culture are promoted faster.
- ✓ Those who **challenge leadership** or question inefficient systems are labeled as "difficult."
- ✓ Being a **"team player"** often means **agreeing rather than pushing for better solutions.**

◈ The Stubborn Innovators Who Refused to Comply

- **Steve Jobs was fired from his own company for being relentless about product perfection.** He returned later, transforming Apple into a global giant.
- **Elon Musk ignored every expert who told him electric cars would never work.** Today, Tesla leads the EV market.
- **Rosa Parks refused to move from her seat, sparking the Civil Rights Movement.** Sometimes, one act of defiance changes everything.

Takeaway: *True innovation requires stubbornness. The world doesn't progress by following rules—it progresses by breaking them.*

Phase 2: The Psychology of Stubbornness—Why Some People Refuse to Give Up

If society discourages stubbornness, why do some people still persist?

1. The Science of Stubbornness

🧠 **Studies show that stubborn individuals:**

- ✓ **Have stronger dopamine responses to challenges.**
- ✓ **Process failure as feedback, not rejection.**
- ✓ **Are less influenced by social pressure.**

💡 **Example:** Two business owners face financial failure.

- **Owner A gives up, believing they weren't meant for success.**
- **Owner B sees failure as a stepping stone and pushes forward.**

◈ **The difference?** Stubbornness.

2. Purpose-Driven vs. Ego-Driven Stubbornness

✔ **Purpose-driven stubbornness fuels innovation.**

✕ **Ego-driven stubbornness prevents growth.**

💡 **Example:**

- **Jeff Bezos was purpose-driven when he kept Amazon alive despite losses for years.**
- **A leader refusing to listen to better ideas is ego-driven.**

◈ **Lesson:** *Know when to hold your ground and when to pivot.*

Phase 3: How to Transform Stubbornness into a Strength

1. Use Stubbornness as Fuel for Rejection

✔ **Every great success story includes rejection.**

💡 **Example:** Walt Disney was rejected **300+ times** before funding Disneyland.

2. Stand by Your Beliefs When Others Doubt You

✔ **The world often doubts what it doesn't yet understand.**

3. Push Forward When Challenges Arise

✔ **Edison, Jordan, Oprah, and Musk all refused to quit.**

💡 **Takeaway:** *The world belongs to those who persist longer than anyone else.*

Conclusion: Own Your Stubbornness

✔ Stubbornness isn't a flaw—it's a choice.

✔ You can use it as **a force for success** or let society convince you it's a weakness.

🚀 **Next Chapter: The Fine Line Between Stubbornness and Recklessness.**

CHAPTER 2

The Fine Line Between Stubbornness and Recklessness

> **"Insanity is doing the same thing over and over again and expecting different results."**
>
> — Albert Einstein

Introduction: The Double-Edged Sword of Stubbornness

Stubbornness is a **powerful tool**, but like any tool, **it can either build or destroy.**

When used correctly, **stubbornness is determination—it helps you push through obstacles, ignore doubters, and stay focused on your vision.**

When used incorrectly, **stubbornness becomes recklessness—it blinds you to reality, makes you ignore valuable advice, and keeps you stuck in a losing battle.**

This is why **some people succeed because of their stubbornness,** while others **fail because of it.**

The key difference?

✔ **Winners know when to be stubborn and when to adapt.**

✕ **Losers refuse to change, even when it's necessary.**

◈ **Example:**

Two entrepreneurs start businesses.

- **Entrepreneur A** refuses to adapt, convinced their original plan is perfect. They ignore customer feedback, dismiss market trends, and **insist on doing things "their way."** Their business collapses.
- **Entrepreneur B** is just as stubborn about success—but they **adapt their strategy when needed,** learning from mistakes instead of repeating them. Their business thrives.

💡 **Lesson: Success doesn't come from refusing to change—it comes from knowing what to change and what to hold firm on.**

In this chapter, we'll explore **the fine line between stubbornness and recklessness, how to avoid falling into the trap of blind persistence, and how to use stubbornness strategically to achieve real success.**

Phase 1: Understanding the Difference Between Stubbornness and Recklessness

Many people confuse **stubbornness** with **determination.**

But **not all persistence is good.**

✔ **Determination means pushing through obstacles intelligently.**

✕ **Recklessness means refusing to change, even when it's obvious you should.**

1. The Key Differences Between Stubbornness and Recklessness

Stubbornness (Productive)	Recklessness (Destructive)
Driven by a clear purpose.	Driven by ego or fear of being wrong.
Open to feedback but holds onto core vision.	Ignores advice, even when it's valuable.
Knows when to pivot and adjust strategy.	Keeps doing the same thing, expecting different results.
Learns from mistakes and failures.	Repeats failures instead of adapting.
Understands the bigger picture.	Gets stuck in the moment, refusing to adjust.

◈ **Example: The Titanic vs. NASA's Apollo Mission**

- The **Titanic's captain ignored multiple iceberg warnings,** convinced the ship was "unsinkable." His **reckless stubbornness led to disaster.**
- The **NASA engineers during Apollo 13 faced a crisis in space.** Instead of insisting on their original plan, they **quickly adapted, adjusted strategies, and saved lives.**

💡 **Lesson:** *Being stubborn about success is great. Being stubborn about failure is foolish.*

2. When Stubbornness Turns Into Self-Sabotage

Sometimes, we're so **emotionally invested** in our ideas that we refuse to see when they're failing.

✔ **You've spent too much time, energy, or money to quit now.**

✔ **You don't want to admit you were wrong.**

✔ **You feel like quitting means failure, even when pivoting would be smarter.**

◈ **Example: Blockbuster vs. Netflix**

- **Blockbuster refused to evolve** because they were stubborn about their traditional business model.
- **Netflix adapted, pivoted, and revolutionized the industry.**
- **Result?** Blockbuster is dead. Netflix is a global giant.

💡 **Lesson:** *Being wrong isn't the problem—refusing to change is.*

Phase 2: The Science Behind Why We Cling to Losing Strategies

🔬 **Why do people hold onto bad decisions, even when the evidence tells them to change?**

1. **The Sunk Cost Fallacy** – "I've already invested too much to quit now."
2. **Cognitive Dissonance** – "If I change my mind, it means I was wrong before."
3. **Fear of Looking Weak** – "If I pivot, people will think I failed."

How to Overcome These Mental Traps

✔ **Reframe quitting as strategic adjustment, not failure.**

✔ **Ask: If I were starting from scratch, would I make the same decision?**

✔ **Focus on long-term success, not short-term pride.**

💡 **Example: Jeff Bezos and Amazon's Failures**

- **Bezos launched multiple failed ventures** (Amazon Fire Phone, auctions, Amazon Wallet).
- Instead of holding onto them, **he cut losses quickly and reinvested in better opportunities.**
- **Result?** Amazon became one of the most successful companies in history.

◈ **Lesson:** *Smart leaders pivot, stubborn people sink.*

Phase 3: How to Be Stubborn About the Right Things

Instead of being stubborn about **your way of doing things,** be stubborn about **your vision,** and flexible about **your strategy.**

◈ **Three Key Areas Where You Should Be Stubborn**

✔ **1. Be Stubborn About Your Goals, But Flexible With Your Methods.**

✔ **2. Be Stubborn About Your Core Values, But Open to New Perspectives.**

✔ **3. Be Stubborn About Your Growth, But Willing to Learn From Failure.**

1. When to Hold Your Ground vs. When to Pivot

Hold Your Ground When...	Pivot When...
Your mission aligns with long-term success.	You're clinging to a failing plan.
The criticism is baseless.	The criticism comes from experts who see a flaw.
The obstacles are external but the vision is strong.	The obstacles are **proving that your method doesn't work.**
You're making measurable progress.	You've hit a dead end with no results.

💡 **Example: Henry Ford vs. Nokia**

- **Henry Ford refused to abandon his vision of affordable cars—but he adapted the way he manufactured them.**
- **Nokia stubbornly stuck to outdated mobile phone designs and lost to Apple.**

◈ **Lesson: "Be stubborn about where you want to go, but be flexible about how you get there."**

2. The Smart Stubbornness Test

Before holding your ground, ask:

❓ **Does this move me closer to my ultimate goal?**

❓ **Am I rejecting advice out of ego or wisdom?**

❓ **If someone else were in my shoes, what would I advise them to do?**

❓ **Am I making progress or just repeating mistakes?**

💡 **If you answer "no" to any of these, it's time to pivot.**

Conclusion: Mastering the Art of Smart Stubbornness

💡 **The key to success isn't refusing to quit—it's knowing when to change.**

✔ **Winners are stubborn about vision, but flexible about strategy.**

✔ **Losers are stubborn about their method, even when it's failing.**

🚀 **The smartest people in history weren't the ones who never changed.**

They were the ones who **knew exactly what to change and when.**

Final Takeaway

🔷 **Be relentless in your pursuit of success, but adaptable in your execution.**

🔷 **Be confident in your ideas, but humble enough to improve them.**

🔷 **Be fearless in your goals, but smart enough to pivot when needed.**

💡 *"The world rewards those who never give up—but only when they know what's worth holding onto."*

🚀 **Next Chapter: How to Use Stubbornness as a Tool for Success.**

CHAPTER 3

How to Use Stubbornness as a Tool for Success

"Stubbornness can either be your greatest asset or your greatest liability. The difference lies in how you use it."

Introduction: Turning Stubbornness Into a Superpower

Stubbornness often gets a bad reputation, but **it's not inherently good or bad—it's a tool.**

✔ Like a hammer, it can either build or destroy.

✔ Like fire, it can either warm your home or burn it down.

The key is **knowing how to control and direct it.**

💡 **Stubbornness isn't about refusing to change—it's about refusing to quit on things that matter.**

In this chapter, we'll explore:

1. How to harness stubbornness for success without letting it derail you.
2. Practical strategies to channel your stubbornness into progress.
3. Real-world examples of individuals who turned their stubbornness into a superpower.

Phase 1: Redefining Stubbornness as a Strategic Tool

1. Stubbornness vs. Resilience

While they may seem similar, **stubbornness and resilience have different outcomes.**

✔ **Stubbornness is unyielding persistence** in the face of opposition.

✔ **Resilience is the ability to adapt, bounce back, and keep moving forward.**

◈ **Stubbornness is what drives you to push forward. Resilience is what helps you recover when you fall.**

💡 **Key Insight:** You need **both stubbornness and resilience** to succeed.

- Stubbornness keeps you focused on your goal.
- Resilience ensures you don't break when challenges arise.

2. The Power of Purpose-Driven Stubbornness

Stubbornness becomes a **force for success** when it's tied to a deeper purpose.

💡 **Ask Yourself:**

1️⃣ **Why is this goal important to me?**

2️⃣ **Does this align with my long-term vision?**

3️⃣ **Am I pursuing this for a meaningful reason—or just out of pride?**

◈ **Example:**

- **Malala Yousafzai refused to back down on her right to education.** Her stubbornness wasn't about ego—it was about a purpose far greater than herself.
- **Thomas Edison was purpose-driven in his pursuit of creating a lightbulb.** He wasn't stubborn for personal pride—he believed in revolutionizing the world.

💡 **Lesson:** Tie your stubbornness to a mission that matters.

3. The Strategic Stubbornness Mindset

To use stubbornness effectively, you must **direct it strategically.**

✔ Be stubborn about your **goals, values, and vision.**

✔ Be flexible about your **methods, strategies, and timeline.**

◈ **Key Principles:**

1. **Separate your vision from your approach.**
   - *The goal is non-negotiable, but the way you achieve it should be adaptable.*
2. **Filter criticism.**
   - *Ignore baseless opinions, but welcome constructive feedback.*
3. **Focus on progress, not perfection.**
   - *Don't let pride stop you from adjusting your course if needed.*

💡 **Takeaway:** Stubbornness works when it's tied to a clear, meaningful direction and balanced with flexibility.

Phase 2: Practical Strategies for Using Stubbornness as a Tool

1. Use Stubbornness to Break Through Rejection

Rejection is inevitable—but **stubborn people turn "no" into fuel for "yes."**

✔ **Every successful person has faced rejection.**

✔ The difference is how they respond to it.

💡 **Examples of Stubborn Persistence:**

- **Walt Disney was rejected by over 300 investors** before securing funding for Disneyland.
- **Colonel Sanders heard "no" more than 1,000 times** before creating KFC.
- **J.K. Rowling's Harry Potter manuscript was rejected by 12 publishers** before becoming a global phenomenon.

◈ **How to Use Stubbornness in the Face of Rejection:**

1. **Treat every "no" as a step closer to "yes."**
2. **Learn from rejection without letting it discourage you.**
3. **Stay committed to your goal but flexible in how you achieve it.**

2. Turn Obstacles Into Opportunities

Every obstacle presents a choice:

✗ **Give up and walk away.**

✔ **Persist and find a way forward.**

◈ **Example: Sara Blakely (Founder of Spanx)**

- When Sara pitched her idea for Spanx, she faced countless rejections.
- Instead of quitting, she **used her stubbornness to adapt her approach** and refine her pitch.
- Today, she's one of the youngest self-made billionaires in history.

💡 **Strategy:** When faced with obstacles, ask yourself:

1. **What can I learn from this challenge?**
2. **How can I pivot without abandoning my goal?**

3. **What's one small step I can take forward?**
4. Balance Passion With Practicality

Stubbornness without strategy is just recklessness.

✔ Be passionate about your goals, but back them up with **a solid plan.**

✔ Use logic to complement your emotion.

◈ **Example: Elon Musk**

- Musk's stubbornness drove him to pursue electric cars and space exploration.
- But his success came from combining passion with **calculated risk-taking and strategic planning.**

💡 **Actionable Tips:**

1. **Create a clear roadmap for your goals.**
2. **Identify potential risks and plan for them.**
3. **Be open to feedback from experts—but stay committed to your mission.**

Phase 3: Stubbornness in Action—Real-Life Success Stories

1. Oprah Winfrey: The Power of Stubborn Belief

- Oprah was fired from her first TV job and told she wasn't fit for television.
- Instead of giving up, she **used that rejection as fuel** to create her own path.
- Today, Oprah is one of the most influential media figures in history.

💡 **Lesson:** Stubbornness can turn doubt into dominance.

2. Steve Jobs: Relentless Perfectionism

- Jobs was famously stubborn about product quality. He refused to settle for "good enough."
- His persistence led to **Apple's game-changing innovations,** including the iPhone and MacBook.

💡 **Lesson:** Be stubborn about excellence, not mediocrity.

3. Serena Williams: Stubborn Excellence in Sports

- Serena's rise to become one of the greatest tennis players of all time wasn't easy.
- Critics doubted her, and injuries tested her resilience—but her **stubborn refusal to quit** set her apart.

💡 **Lesson:** Stubbornness can make you a champion—if you stay disciplined.

Phase 4: Exercises to Channel Stubbornness Productively

1. The Stubbornness Audit

✔ Write down a recent time when stubbornness helped you.

✔ Write down a time when it hurt you.

✔ Identify patterns: What made it productive vs. destructive?

2. The Stubbornness Filter

✔ **What am I holding onto that's worth fighting for?**

✔ **What am I holding onto that's holding me back?**

✔ **How can I redirect my stubbornness toward growth?**

3. The "No" Challenge

✔ Set a goal to pursue something and collect 10 rejections.

✔ Use each rejection as an opportunity to refine your approach.

💡 **Lesson:** Every rejection gets you closer to success.

Conclusion: The World Belongs to the Stubborn (When They're Smart About It)

✔ **Stubbornness isn't the enemy of success—it's the foundation of it.**

✔ **But it's only valuable when paired with purpose, strategy, and flexibility.**

💡 *"Be stubborn about your goals, but smart about how you achieve them."*

🚀 **Next Chapter:** The Daily Habits of Purposeful Stubbornness—How to make small, stubborn efforts every day that lead to big success.

CHAPTER 4

The Daily Habits of Purposeful Stubbornness—How to Make Small, Stubborn Efforts Every Day That Lead to Big Success

"Success is the sum of small efforts, repeated day in and day out."

— Robert Collier

Introduction: Why Habits Define Success

The world often glorifies **grand gestures and big wins**, but the reality is this:

💡 **Success is built on small, consistent actions.**

Purposeful stubbornness isn't about a single bold stand—it's about **persistent effort, day after day, even when it feels mundane or thankless.**

✔ **Every bestseller started with a single page written daily.**

✔ **Every championship was won through daily practice.**

✔ **Every business empire began with stubbornly small steps.**

In this chapter, we'll explore:

1. How to cultivate habits that align with purposeful stubbornness.
2. The science behind why small, daily actions compound into massive success.
3. Actionable habits you can implement today to fuel your journey.

Phase 1: The Science of Small, Stubborn Steps

1. Why Small Actions Matter More Than Big Goals

Most people focus on **big goals,** but they forget the power of **small actions.**

✔ A goal sets the direction, but habits are the engine that gets you there.

✔ Big wins are the result of **consistent, stubborn effort.**

◈ **The Compound Effect** – *Small actions, repeated consistently, lead to exponential results over time.*

💡 **Example:**

- If you read 10 pages of a book daily, you'll read 15–20 books a year.
- If you save $5 daily, you'll accumulate $1,800+ in a year, not counting compound interest.
- If you exercise for 20 minutes daily, you'll see significant health improvements within months.

◈ **Lesson:** Don't underestimate the power of showing up daily, even in small ways.

2. The Habit Loop: How Habits Are Formed

According to **James Clear's "Atomic Habits,"** habits form through a simple loop:

1 **Cue** – A trigger that starts the behavior.

2 **Routine** – The behavior itself.

3 **Reward** – The benefit you receive from completing the habit.

How to Apply This:

✔ Identify a cue (e.g., time of day, location).

✔ Build a simple, repeatable routine.

✔ Reward yourself to reinforce the habit.

◈ **Example:**

- **Goal:** Write a book.
- **Cue:** Sit at your desk every morning at 7 AM.
- **Routine:** Write 500 words, no matter what.
- **Reward:** Celebrate completing your session with a cup of coffee or a short walk.

◈ **Lesson:** Habits aren't formed overnight—they're built through repetition and consistency.

3. The Role of Stubbornness in Habit Formation

Stubbornness is your **greatest ally** when it comes to building habits.

✔ It helps you show up **even when you don't feel like it.**

✔ It pushes you through the **initial discomfort** of forming a new habit.

✔ It keeps you consistent, even when results aren't immediate.

💡 **Example:**

- **Stephen King writes every day, even on holidays.** His stubborn commitment to the craft is why he's one of the most prolific authors in history.
- **Kobe Bryant famously practiced at 4 AM daily, even when others slept.** His stubborn work ethic turned him into an NBA legend.

◈ **Lesson:** Stubbornness helps you stay disciplined when motivation fades.

Phase 2: Daily Habits of Purposeful Stubbornness

1. Start With One Small, Non-Negotiable Habit

✔ Choose one habit that aligns with your long-term goal.

✔ Make it so small that it's impossible to fail.

💡 **Examples of Small, Stubborn Habits:**

- Write 100 words a day for your book.
- Save $1 a day toward your financial goals.
- Do 10 push-ups daily to improve fitness.

◈ **Why It Works:**

✔ Small habits are easy to stick with, but they snowball into significant progress over time.

2. Commit to Showing Up Every Day (No Matter What)

The key to purposeful stubbornness is **consistency.**

✔ Show up even when you don't feel like it.

✔ Show up even when progress feels slow.

✔ Show up even when you doubt yourself.

💡 **Example:** Jerry Seinfeld's "Don't Break the Chain" Method

- Seinfeld committed to writing jokes every single day.
- He marked each successful day with an "X" on a calendar, creating an unbroken chain of effort.
- His stubborn consistency helped him become one of the most successful comedians of all time.

◈ **Action Step:** Get a calendar and track your daily habit streak. Your goal? **Don't break the chain.**

3. Focus on Process, Not Perfection

✔ Success isn't about doing things perfectly—it's about **doing them consistently.**

✔ Stubborn people focus on the **process** rather than obsessing over immediate results.

💡 **Example:** Olympic athletes train for years, focusing on daily improvement, not immediate victories.

◈ **Action Step:** Track your habits, but don't judge yourself for small setbacks. Progress, not perfection, is the goal.

Phase 3: Real-Life Stories of Purposeful Daily Stubbornness

1. James Dyson: Stubborn Innovation

- Dyson created 5,126 failed prototypes before inventing the world's first bagless vacuum cleaner.
- His daily habit? **Tinkering, testing, and refining—every single day.**

💡 **Lesson:** Success isn't about one breakthrough—it's about consistent effort over time.

2. Maya Angelou: Stubborn Creativity

- Angelou wrote every morning, no matter how she felt.
- Her daily habit of showing up led to some of the most impactful works of literature.

💡 **Lesson:** Creativity flows when you commit to the routine.

3. Elon Musk: Stubborn Experimentation

- Musk's schedule involves daily testing, learning, and iterating—whether it's rockets or electric cars.

💡 **Lesson:** Small, stubborn experiments lead to massive innovation.

Phase 4: Exercises to Build Daily Habits of Purposeful Stubbornness

1. The "1% Better" Challenge

✔ Commit to improving by just 1% every day in one area of your life.

💡 **Example:** Write 1% more words, save 1% more money, or do 1% more push-ups.

2. The Five-Minute Rule

✔ When you don't feel like doing something, commit to just five minutes.

💡 **Why It Works:** Five minutes often turns into much more once you start.

3. The Stubborn Accountability System

✔ Partner with someone who will hold you accountable for your daily habits.

✔ Share your progress and challenges with them weekly.

Conclusion: Small Steps, Big Success

✔ **Stubbornness is what keeps you moving forward, one step at a time.**

✔ **Habits are the building blocks of success.**

✔ **When you combine stubbornness with small, daily efforts, you create unstoppable momentum.**

💡 *"The difference between ordinary and extraordinary is the stubborn refusal to stop showing up every day."*

🚀 **Next Chapter:** The Stubborn Mindset of the World's Greatest Achievers—How to think like those who refuse to give up.

CHAPTER 5

The Stubborn Mindset of the World's Greatest Achievers—How to Think Like Those Who Refuse to Give Up

> **"Whether you think you can, or you think you can't—you're right."**
>
> — Henry Ford

Introduction: The Power of a Stubborn Mindset

Behind every groundbreaking success story lies one common denominator: **a mindset that refuses to quit.**

✔ **Winners aren't always the smartest, fastest, or most talented.**

✔ **They're the ones who refuse to stop when the odds are stacked against them.**

The world's greatest achievers—from inventors to athletes, entrepreneurs to activists—all share a common trait: **a stubborn, unyielding belief in themselves and their goals.**

This chapter dives deep into the **psychology and mindset** of those who persist against all odds. By understanding how they think, you can adopt their mindset and apply it to your own life.

Phase 1: The Core Beliefs of Stubborn Achievers

1. Belief #1: Obstacles Are Temporary, Not Permanent

◈ **The Mindset Shift:**

- Most people see obstacles as stop signs.
- Stubborn achievers see them as detours—temporary delays, not permanent barriers.

💡 **Example:**

- **Thomas Edison viewed every failed lightbulb prototype as a step closer to success.**
- Instead of saying, "This is impossible," he asked, *"What did I learn, and how can I improve?"*

◈ **Actionable Insight:**

✔ When you face an obstacle, ask yourself:

- *"Is this a true failure or just a lesson?"*
- *"How can I use this setback to grow stronger?"*

2. Belief #2: Progress Is More Important Than Perfection

◈ **The Mindset Shift:**

- Perfectionists wait for the "perfect" moment or idea.
- Stubborn achievers act, knowing that progress—no matter how small—is what matters.

💡 **Example:**

- **Jeff Bezos launched Amazon as a simple online bookstore, knowing it wasn't perfect.** Over time, he stubbornly improved it, turning it into the e-commerce giant we know today.

◈ **Actionable Insight:**

✔ Focus on taking consistent, small steps rather than waiting for ideal conditions.

✔ Ask yourself: *"What's one thing I can do today to move forward?"*

3. Belief #3: Rejection Is Just Redirection

◈ **The Mindset Shift:**

- Most people internalize rejection as failure.
- Stubborn achievers see rejection as feedback and a chance to pivot.

💡 **Example:**

- **Oprah Winfrey was fired from her first TV job and told she wasn't fit for television.** Instead of giving up, she redirected her efforts and built her own platform, becoming one of the most influential media figures in history.

◈ **Actionable Insight:**

✔ Treat every rejection as a stepping stone, not a roadblock.

✔ Ask yourself: *"What can I learn from this, and how can I adjust my approach?"*

Phase 2: The Psychological Foundations of Stubborn Achievers

1. Grit: The Key Ingredient for Long-Term Success

🔬 **Research Insight:**

Angela Duckworth, author of *Grit: The Power of Passion and Perseverance*, found that grit—not talent—is the strongest predictor of success.

💡 **Key Takeaway:**

✔ Stubborn achievers aren't necessarily more talented—they're just more persistent.

◈ **Action Step:**

Build grit by focusing on:

1 **Passion:** Align your stubbornness with what truly excites you.

2 **Perseverance:** Commit to showing up, even when motivation fades.

2. Self-Efficacy: Believing You Can Shape Your Future

🔬 **Psychological Insight:**

- People with high self-efficacy believe their actions directly influence outcomes.
- This belief fuels their stubbornness—they trust their ability to figure things out.

💡 **Example:**

- **Serena Williams believed in her ability to win, even when critics doubted her.** That belief drove her relentless work ethic and record-breaking success.

◈ **Action Step:**

✔ Build self-efficacy by celebrating small wins and reminding yourself of past successes.

3. Growth Mindset: Turning Failure Into Fuel

Carol Dweck's Research:

- People with a growth mindset see failure as an opportunity to grow.
- Stubborn achievers embody this mindset—they use failure as a stepping stone, not a stopping point.

Example:

- **Michael Jordan famously said, "I've missed more than 9,000 shots in my career. I've failed over and over again. And that is why I succeed."**

Action Step:

✔ After every setback, ask: *"What did I learn, and how can I improve?"*

Phase 3: The Daily Practices of a Stubborn Mindset

1. Visualize Success Daily

✔ Stubborn achievers have a clear vision of what they want—and they revisit it every day.

Example:

- **Arnold Schwarzenegger visualized himself as a champion bodybuilder long before he won his first title.**

Action Step:

✔ Spend 5 minutes daily visualizing your ultimate goal.

✔ Imagine yourself overcoming obstacles and succeeding.

2. Practice Gratitude for the Journey

✔ Gratitude keeps stubborn achievers grounded and motivated.

✔ Instead of focusing only on the end goal, they appreciate the small wins along the way.

💡 **Example:**

- **Tony Robbins starts every day by practicing gratitude, which fuels his energy and drive.**

◈ **Action Step:**

✔ Write down three things you're grateful for every morning.

3. Surround Yourself With the Right People

✔ Stubborn achievers surround themselves with people who challenge and inspire them.

✔ They avoid negativity and seek out those who fuel their vision.

💡 **Example:**

- **Walt Disney's success was partly due to his brother Roy, who helped turn dreams into reality.**

◈ **Action Step:**

✔ Identify one person who motivates you and spend more time with them.

Phase 4: Exercises to Build a Stubborn Mindset

1. The "What If" Exercise

✔ Write down your biggest goal and list every reason why it might fail.

✔ Next to each reason, write a potential solution.

💡 **Lesson:** This shifts your mindset from fear of failure to problem-solving.

2. The "10-Year Vision" Exercise

✔ Imagine your life 10 years from now if you stubbornly pursued your goals.

✔ Write down the details: What would your career, relationships, and health look like?

💡 **Lesson:** A vivid vision fuels your stubborn drive.

Conclusion: Adopting the Stubborn Mindset

✔ **The world's greatest achievers aren't the ones who never failed—they're the ones who never stopped.**

✔ **Their stubborn mindset is their superpower.**

💡 *"To achieve greatness, you don't need to be the best—you just need to be the one who refuses to give up."*

🚀 **Next Chapter:** Stubborn Leadership: How to Lead With an Unwavering Vision and Inspire Others.

CHAPTER 6

Stubborn Leadership—How to Lead With an Unwavering Vision and Inspire Others

> **"A leader is one who knows the way, goes the way, and shows the way."**
>
> — John C. Maxwell

Introduction: Leadership Requires Stubbornness

Great leaders aren't just skilled—they're **stubborn.**

✔ They stick to their vision, even when the path forward isn't clear.

✔ They inspire others to believe in possibilities others consider impossible.

✔ They know when to hold their ground and when to adapt.

But stubborn leadership isn't about being inflexible or dictatorial—it's about being **resilient, strategic, and inspiring.**

💡 **Leadership isn't about always being right. It's about being steadfast in your purpose while remaining adaptable in your methods.**

In this chapter, we'll explore:

1. How to use purposeful stubbornness to lead effectively.
2. How to balance strong leadership with adaptability.
3. Real-world examples of stubborn leaders who changed the world.

Phase 1: The Core Traits of Stubborn Leaders

1. Visionary Thinking: Seeing What Others Don't

◈ **Stubborn leaders are driven by a clear vision.**

- They see opportunities where others see obstacles.
- They remain focused on the long-term, even when the present is filled with challenges.

💡 **Example:**

- **Martin Luther King Jr. refused to abandon his dream of equality, even in the face of immense resistance.** His unwavering vision inspired millions to join the Civil Rights Movement.

◈ **Actionable Insight:**

✔ As a leader, ask yourself: *"What is the big picture I'm working toward? How can I communicate it to others?"*

2. Emotional Resilience: Staying Calm Under Pressure

◈ **Leadership is stressful, but stubborn leaders thrive under pressure.**

- They don't let setbacks derail their confidence.
- They remain composed, using challenges as opportunities to grow.

💡 **Example:**

- **Angela Merkel's calm, steady leadership during the European financial crisis earned her global respect.**

◈ **Actionable Insight:**

✔ Build emotional resilience by practicing mindfulness and focusing on solutions, not problems.

3. Empathy: Inspiring Others to Believe

◈ **Stubborn leaders don't just lead by force—they inspire by connecting with their teams.**

- They understand their team's struggles and use empathy to build trust.
- They balance stubbornness with compassion, ensuring others feel heard and valued.

💡 **Example:**

- **Jacinda Ardern, New Zealand's Prime Minister, led with empathy during crises, earning global admiration.**

◈ **Actionable Insight:**

✔ Regularly ask your team for feedback and show genuine interest in their concerns.

Phase 2: Balancing Stubbornness and Flexibility in Leadership

1. When to Be Stubborn: Defend Your Vision

✔ **Hold your ground when your principles or mission are at stake.**

✔ Stubbornness shows your team that you believe in your vision, even when others doubt it.

💡 **Example:**

- **Elon Musk faced criticism for pursuing reusable rockets.** Instead of backing down, he doubled down—and SpaceX revolutionized space travel.

◈ **Actionable Insight:**

✔ Clearly define your non-negotiables: What are the core values or goals you will never compromise on?

2. When to Be Flexible: Adapt Your Strategy

✔ **Flexibility doesn't mean abandoning your vision—it means finding better ways to achieve it.**

✔ Great leaders are stubborn about the destination but open to different routes.

💡 **Example:**

- **Reed Hastings, CEO of Netflix, pivoted from DVD rentals to streaming, then to content creation.** His adaptability kept Netflix ahead of its competition.

◈ **Actionable Insight:**

✔ Regularly evaluate your strategy and ask: *"Is this the best way to achieve my goal?"*

3. The Balance Formula: Lead With Conviction and Openness

Be Stubborn When...	Be Flexible When...
Your vision aligns with your long-term goals.	Your current approach isn't delivering results.
Criticism comes from naysayers or skeptics.	Feedback comes from trusted advisors or experts.
The obstacle is external and surmountable.	The obstacle requires a fundamental change.

💡 **Lesson:** Great leaders **know when to fight and when to adapt.**

Phase 3: Stubborn Leadership in Action—Real-World Examples

1. Steve Jobs: Stubborn About Perfection

- Jobs refused to settle for "good enough" products, insisting on excellence.
- His stubborn leadership resulted in iconic innovations like the iPhone and MacBook.

💡 **Lesson:** Be stubborn about quality—it sets you apart.

2. Nelson Mandela: Stubborn About Justice

- Mandela spent 27 years in prison but never abandoned his vision of equality and freedom.
- His stubborn leadership united a divided nation and ended apartheid.

💡 **Lesson:** Stubborn leadership inspires others to fight for a shared cause.

3. Indra Nooyi: Stubborn About Innovation

- As CEO of PepsiCo, Nooyi pushed for healthier product lines, despite initial resistance.
- Her stubborn vision transformed the company and future-proofed its growth.

💡 **Lesson:** Stubborn leadership involves making tough, forward-thinking decisions.

Phase 4: Exercises to Cultivate Stubborn Leadership

1. The Vision Statement Exercise

✔ Write down your vision in one sentence.

✔ Ask yourself: *"How can I make this clear, inspiring, and actionable for my team?"*

2. The Feedback Balance Sheet

✔ List the feedback you've received as a leader.

✔ Separate constructive feedback from baseless criticism.

✔ Use this sheet to decide when to adapt and when to stand firm.

3. The Resilience Challenge

✔ Identify one leadership challenge you're currently facing.

✔ Commit to tackling it with calm determination over the next 30 days.

Conclusion: The Stubborn Leader's Legacy

✔ **Leadership isn't about being perfect—it's about being persistent.**

✔ **Stubborn leaders inspire others by standing firm in their vision while remaining adaptable in their approach.**

💡 *"The best leaders aren't the loudest or the smartest—they're the ones who refuse to give up on what matters most."*

🚀 **Next Chapter:** Handling Rejection and Failure Like a Stubborn Achiever—How to turn every "no" into a stepping stone to success.

CHAPTER 7

Handling Rejection and Failure Like a Stubborn Achiever—How to Turn Every "No" Into a Stepping Stone to Success

"I have not failed. I've just found 10,000 ways that won't work."

— Thomas Edison

Introduction: Why Rejection and Failure Are Necessary

Rejection and failure are **inevitable parts of the journey to success.**

✔ Every bestseller was rejected before it was published.

✔ Every breakthrough idea was ridiculed before it was celebrated.

✔ Every great leader faced countless setbacks before achieving their vision.

The difference between those who succeed and those who don't isn't the absence of failure—it's **how they respond to it.**

Stubborn achievers don't let rejection or failure define them. Instead, they:

1. Use rejection as fuel to improve.
2. Treat failure as feedback, not a verdict.
3. Stay relentless in their pursuit of success.

This chapter will explore how to:

1. Reframe rejection and failure as opportunities.
2. Build resilience to keep going when the world says "no."
3. Develop practical strategies to turn setbacks into stepping stones.

Phase 1: Reframing Rejection and Failure

1. Rejection Isn't Personal—It's a Test of Persistence

◈ **The Mindset Shift:**

- Most people see rejection as a reflection of their worth.
- Stubborn achievers see rejection as part of the process.

💡 **Example:**

- **J.K. Rowling's Harry Potter manuscript was rejected by 12 publishers.** She didn't take it personally—she saw it as one step closer to finding the right fit.

◈ **Actionable Insight:**

✔ When faced with rejection, remind yourself: *"This isn't about me—it's about finding the right opportunity."*

2. Failure Is Feedback, Not a Dead End

◈ **The Mindset Shift:**

- Most people see failure as the end of the road.
- Stubborn achievers see failure as valuable feedback to improve their approach.

💡 **Example:**

- **Dyson created 5,126 prototypes before inventing the bagless vacuum cleaner.** Each failure taught him what didn't work, bringing him closer to success.

◈ **Actionable Insight:**

✔ After every failure, ask yourself:

- *"What did I learn?"*
- *"How can I apply this lesson to my next attempt?"*

3. Embrace the Growth Mindset

🔬 **Research Insight:**

- People with a growth mindset believe that abilities can be developed through effort.
- They see failure as an opportunity to grow, not a sign of inadequacy.

💡 **Example:**

- **Michael Jordan missed over 9,000 shots in his career, but he viewed every missed shot as a step toward improvement.**

◈ **Actionable Insight:**

✔ Cultivate a growth mindset by focusing on learning, not perfection.

Phase 2: Building Resilience to Rejection and Failure

1. Develop Emotional Resilience

✔ Emotional resilience helps you bounce back from setbacks without losing motivation.

💡 **Strategies for Building Emotional Resilience:**

1️⃣ **Detach Emotionally From Rejection:** Treat it as a business decision, not a personal attack.

2️⃣ **Practice Gratitude:** Focus on what's going well in your life to maintain perspective.

3️⃣ **Find Your "Why":** A clear purpose makes it easier to endure setbacks.

2. Create a Failure Log

✔ A failure log helps you track setbacks and identify patterns for growth.

💡 **How to Create a Failure Log:**

1️⃣ **Write down the failure.**

2️⃣ **Note what went wrong.**

3️⃣ **Identify what you learned.**

4️⃣ **Plan your next steps.**

◈ **Example:**

- **Thomas Edison's notebooks were filled with failed experiments, each one documented to refine his process.**

3. Rejection Challenge: Desensitize Yourself to "No"

✔ The more you face rejection, the less intimidating it becomes.

💡 **Actionable Challenge:**

- Set a goal to collect 10 rejections this month (e.g., pitch ideas, ask for opportunities).
- Celebrate each "no" as progress toward resilience.

◈ **Lesson:** Rejection becomes less scary when you normalize it.

Phase 3: Turning Setbacks Into Stepping Stones

1. Analyze Rejection Objectively

✔ Instead of reacting emotionally, analyze why you were rejected.

💡 **Key Questions to Ask:**

1️⃣ *"Was this rejection due to factors I can control?"*

2️⃣ *"What feedback can I use to improve?"*

3️⃣ *"What's my next move?"*

◈ **Example:**

- **Howard Schultz's idea for Starbucks was rejected by 200+ investors.** He used their feedback to refine his pitch and eventually built a global brand.

2. Focus on the Long Game

✔ Rejection and failure are temporary, but your vision is long-term.

💡 **Example:**

- **Walt Disney was fired from a newspaper for "lacking creativity."** Instead of giving up, he persisted, eventually creating one of the most iconic brands in history.

◈ **Actionable Insight:**

✔ Ask yourself: *"Will this matter in 5 years? What can I do today to keep moving forward?"*

3. Celebrate Small Wins

✔ Small victories keep you motivated during challenging times.

💡 **Example:**

- **Serena Williams celebrated every small improvement during training, which fueled her drive to become the greatest tennis player of all time.**

◈ **Actionable Insight:**

✔ Create a "win journal" to track daily achievements, no matter how small.

Phase 4: Real-Life Stories of Rejection and Resilience

1. Oprah Winfrey: Fired but Unstoppable

- Oprah was fired from her first TV job but refused to let it define her.
- Her resilience and vision led to the creation of a media empire.

💡 **Lesson:** Rejection is just redirection.

2. Steven Spielberg: Rejected by Film School

- Spielberg was rejected from film school multiple times but didn't let that stop him.
- He stubbornly pursued his passion and became one of the greatest filmmakers of all time.

💡 **Lesson:** Don't let gatekeepers dictate your destiny.

3. Soichiro Honda: Failure Turned to Fortune

- Honda was rejected from a job at Toyota, but he used the setback to start his own company.
- Today, Honda is a global leader in the automotive industry.

💡 **Lesson:** Every "no" is an opportunity to create your own "yes."

Phase 5: Exercises to Master Rejection and Failure

1. The Failure Autopsy

✔ Write down your biggest failure and analyze:

1️⃣ What went wrong?

2️⃣ What lessons did I learn?

3️⃣ What changes will I make moving forward?

2. The "Rejection Is Progress" Tracker

✔ Create a tracker to celebrate every rejection as a step closer to success.

✔ Reward yourself for hitting rejection milestones (e.g., 10 rejections = a treat).

3. The Resilience Ritual

✔ Start each day with a mantra: *"Every setback is a setup for a comeback."*

✔ End each day by reflecting on what you learned and how you grew.

Conclusion: The Gift of Rejection and Failure

✔ **Rejection and failure aren't roadblocks—they're stepping stones.**

✔ **Every "no" brings you closer to the right "yes."**

💡 *"Success isn't about avoiding failure—it's about refusing to stop after failing."*

🚀 **Next Chapter:** Knowing When to Pivot—The Art of Adaptation Without Giving Up.

CHAPTER 8

Knowing When to Pivot—The Art of Adaptation Without Giving Up

"Fall seven times, stand up eight."

— Japanese Proverb

Introduction: The Balance Between Persistence and Flexibility

Stubbornness is a **powerful asset**, but **blind persistence can lead to failure.**

✔ The most successful people aren't just persistent—they're adaptable.

✔ They know when to push forward and when to pivot.

✔ They refuse to give up on their goals but are willing to change their approach.

💡 **Knowing when to pivot isn't giving up—it's leveling up.**

In this chapter, we'll explore:

1. How to recognize the signs that it's time to pivot.
2. How to adapt your strategy while staying true to your vision.
3. Real-world examples of successful pivots that led to massive breakthroughs.

Phase 1: Recognizing When to Pivot

1. The Signs That It's Time for a Change

Sometimes, **stubbornly sticking to a failing plan can hold you back.**

◈ **Key Signs You Need to Pivot:**

1️⃣ **You're hitting a dead end repeatedly.**

- Despite your efforts, progress has stalled.

2️⃣ **Your strategy isn't aligned with your long-term vision.**

- The path you're on doesn't feel right anymore.

3️⃣ **Feedback reveals flaws you can't ignore.**

- Trusted advisors or customers suggest significant changes.

4️⃣ **You're no longer passionate about the process.**

- Burnout or disinterest signals a need for a new direction.

💡 **Example:**

- **Blockbuster stubbornly stuck to its DVD rental model, ignoring the rise of streaming.** Netflix, on the other hand, pivoted early, dominating the industry.

◈ **Lesson:** *Refusing to pivot when needed can be the difference between success and irrelevance.*

2. The Emotional Barriers to Pivoting

✔ **The Sunk Cost Fallacy:**

- You've invested so much time, money, or energy that you feel quitting would waste it all.

✔ **Fear of Judgment:**

- You're afraid of what others will think if you change direction.

✔ **Ego and Pride:**

- Admitting your strategy isn't working feels like admitting failure.

💡 **How to Overcome These Barriers:**

1️⃣ **Reframe quitting as evolving.**

2️⃣ **Focus on the long-term benefits of adapting.**

3️⃣ **Remind yourself: Successful people don't cling to mistakes—they learn from them.**

Phase 2: The Art of Pivoting Without Losing Focus

1. Stay True to Your Vision, But Change Your Approach

✔ **The Goal Remains Constant:**

- Your mission or vision doesn't change—it's the strategy that evolves.

💡 **Example:**

- **Slack started as a gaming company but pivoted to focus on team communication software.** Today, it's one of the most popular workplace tools.

🔷 **Lesson:** Be stubborn about the destination but flexible about the route.

2. Embrace Data-Driven Decisions

✔ Successful pivots are based on evidence, not guesswork.

💡 **How to Pivot Strategically:**

1 **Analyze results:** What's working, and what's not?

2 **Listen to feedback:** What are customers or stakeholders saying?

3 **Test new ideas:** Experiment before fully committing to a new path.

◈ **Example:**

- **YouTube started as a dating site before pivoting to a video-sharing platform after noticing user behavior.**

◈ **Lesson:** Let data, not emotion, guide your decisions.

3. Break Down the Pivot Process

◈ **Steps to Pivot Successfully:**

1 **Acknowledge the need for change.**

2 **Define what stays the same (your vision).**

3 **Identify what needs to change (strategy, audience, product).**

4 **Communicate the pivot clearly to your team or stakeholders.**

5 **Execute the pivot in phases, testing and iterating as you go.**

💡 **Example:**

- **Instagram started as a location-based app before pivoting to focus solely on photo sharing.** This shift made it one of the most successful social media platforms in the world.

Phase 3: Real-Life Stories of Successful Pivots

1. Howard Schultz: Pivoting Starbucks

- Starbucks started as a coffee bean retailer. Schultz envisioned it as a coffeehouse experience, creating the global chain we know today.

💡 **Lesson:** A bold pivot can redefine an entire industry.

2. Twitter: A Pivot Born From Failure

- Twitter started as Odeo, a podcast platform. When Apple launched iTunes Podcasts, Odeo pivoted to microblogging—and Twitter was born.

💡 **Lesson:** Failure can be the perfect opportunity to pivot into something better.

3. Netflix: From Rentals to Streaming

- Netflix pivoted from DVD rentals to streaming, and later to content creation, staying ahead of the curve.

💡 **Lesson:** Staying adaptable allows you to lead, not follow, your industry.

Phase 4: Exercises to Master the Art of Pivoting

1. The Pivot Clarity Worksheet

✔ Write down:

1️⃣ Your ultimate vision.

2️⃣ What's working in your current strategy.

3 What's not working.

4 Potential new strategies to test.

💡 **Lesson:** Clarity helps you pivot with confidence.

2. The "Fresh Perspective" Challenge

✔ Ask three trusted individuals to give feedback on your current approach.

✔ Use their insights to identify blind spots and areas for improvement.

3. The Micro-Pivot Experiment

✔ Test a small change before committing to a full pivot.

✔ Evaluate the results and scale up if successful.

💡 **Lesson:** Small experiments reduce risk and build confidence.

Conclusion: Pivoting Is a Skill, Not a Failure

✔ **Pivoting doesn't mean giving up—it means growing smarter.**

✔ **Stubborn achievers know that adaptation is key to long-term success.**

💡 *"When the path forward is blocked, create a new one. The goal remains—only the strategy changes."*

🚀 **Next Chapter:** The Power of Stubborn Leadership—How to Influence and Motivate Others to Stay the Course.

CHAPTER 9

The Power of Stubborn Leadership—How to Influence and Motivate Others to Stay the Course

"A leader is someone who demonstrates what's possible."

— Mark Yarnell

Introduction: Leadership Is Built on Stubborn Belief

Leadership is not just about personal persistence—it's about inspiring others to believe in a vision and motivating them to stay committed, even in the face of challenges.

✔ **A great leader doesn't just push through obstacles—they bring their team along for the journey.**

✔ **They are stubborn about their vision but flexible in their approach to motivating others.**

In this chapter, we'll explore:

1. How to use your stubbornness to inspire and influence others.
2. Techniques for motivating a team to stay the course during tough times.
3. Real-world examples of leaders who turned their vision into a shared mission.

Phase 1: Stubborn Leadership as a Force for Influence

1. The Leader's Stubborn Vision

◈ **The Foundation of Leadership:**

- People follow leaders who believe in their vision so deeply that it becomes contagious.
- A stubborn leader's unwavering belief inspires others to adopt the same conviction.

💡 **Example:**

- **Dr. Martin Luther King Jr. was stubborn in his pursuit of equality, and his belief ignited a global movement.** His "I Have a Dream" speech transformed his vision into a shared mission.

◈ **Actionable Insight:**

✔ Define your vision in a way that resonates with others.

✔ Ask yourself: *"How can I communicate my belief so strongly that others feel it too?"*

2. The Role of Emotional Intelligence in Leadership

◈ **Why Emotional Intelligence Matters:**

- Stubbornness alone doesn't make a great leader—empathy and understanding do.
- Emotional intelligence helps you connect with your team on a deeper level, making your leadership more effective.

💡 **Example:**

- **Jacinda Ardern's empathetic leadership during crises earned her the trust and loyalty of her people.**

◈ **Actionable Insight:**

✔ Practice active listening. Understand your team's fears, concerns, and motivations.

✔ Show that you care about their success, not just the outcome.

3. The Power of Leading by Example

◈ **Stubborn leaders inspire action through their behavior.**

- When you demonstrate unwavering commitment to your goals, your team will follow suit.

💡 **Example:**

- **Mahatma Gandhi led India's independence movement with nonviolent resistance, showing his followers that persistence and integrity were more powerful than aggression.**

◈ **Actionable Insight:**

✔ Model the behavior you want to see in others.

✔ Be the most committed person in the room.

Phase 2: Motivating Others to Stay the Course

1. Create a Shared Vision

✔ **People are more motivated when they feel they're part of something bigger than themselves.**

💡 **Example:**

- **Elon Musk communicates Tesla's mission to accelerate the world's transition to sustainable energy.** This vision motivates employees and customers alike.

◈ **Actionable Insight:**

✔ Involve your team in defining the mission. Make them feel like co-creators, not followers.

✔ Ask yourself: *"How can I make my vision a shared goal?"*

2. Celebrate Small Wins

✔ **Big goals can feel overwhelming, but small victories keep people motivated.**

💡 **Example:**

- **Jeff Bezos celebrated Amazon's early milestones, like reaching 100 customers, to keep his team inspired.**

◈ **Actionable Insight:**

✔ Break your goals into smaller, achievable milestones.

✔ Celebrate every win—no matter how small.

3. Build Resilience Through Encouragement

✔ **Challenges are inevitable, but how you respond to them sets the tone for your team.**

💡 **Example:**

- **Winston Churchill inspired resilience during WWII with his famous speech: "We shall never surrender."**

◈ **Actionable Insight:**

✔ During tough times, remind your team why the goal matters.

✔ Use setbacks as opportunities to rally and refocus.

Phase 3: Real-World Examples of Stubborn Leadership in Action

1. Nelson Mandela: Inspiring Unity Through Stubborn Belief

- Mandela's unwavering commitment to ending apartheid inspired a nation to unite.
- His leadership was rooted in a stubborn belief in justice and reconciliation.

💡 **Lesson:** A stubborn leader's vision can transform conflict into collaboration.

2. Steve Jobs: Relentless Commitment to Excellence

- Jobs demanded perfection from his team, refusing to compromise on quality.
- His stubborn leadership inspired Apple to create products that changed the world.

💡 **Lesson:** Stubborn leadership raises the standards for everyone around you.

3. Rosa Parks: Leading Through Quiet Defiance

- Rosa Parks' refusal to give up her bus seat sparked a movement.
- Her quiet yet stubborn leadership inspired millions to fight for civil rights.

💡 **Lesson:** Leadership isn't about volume—it's about conviction.

Phase 4: Exercises to Build Stubborn Leadership Skills

1. The Vision Alignment Exercise

✔ Write down your vision.

✔ Share it with your team and ask for their input.

✔ Work together to refine the vision into something everyone believes in.

2. The Empathy Challenge

✔ Schedule one-on-one conversations with team members.

✔ Ask them about their goals, challenges, and suggestions for improvement.

💡 **Lesson:** Connection builds trust, and trust fuels commitment.

3. The Stubborn Role Model Worksheet

✔ Identify a leader you admire for their persistence.

✔ Study their strategies and mindset.

✔ Write down three lessons you can apply to your leadership style.

Conclusion: Stubborn Leadership Creates Lasting Impact

✔ **Stubborn leaders don't just achieve success—they inspire others to achieve it too.**

✔ **Their unwavering vision and resilience create a ripple effect, empowering others to persist.**

💡 *"The best leaders are those who believe so strongly in their vision that others can't help but believe in it too."*

🚀 **Next Chapter:** The Dark Side of Stubbornness—How to Recognize and Avoid Its Pitfalls.

CHAPTER 10

The Dark Side of Stubbornness—How to Recognize and Avoid Its Pitfalls

"Strength lies not in stubbornness, but in knowing when to yield."

— Unknown

Introduction: When Stubbornness Becomes a Weakness

Stubbornness, when used wisely, is a superpower—but when left unchecked, it can lead to **isolation, failure, and missed opportunities.**

✔ **It can blind you to better solutions.**

✔ **It can damage relationships and alienate others.**

✔ **It can trap you in cycles of ego-driven resistance.**

💡 **The key is to recognize when your stubbornness is holding you back and learn how to redirect it.**

This chapter explores:

1. The risks of unchecked stubbornness.
2. How to identify when it's working against you.
3. Strategies to avoid the pitfalls while keeping the benefits.

Phase 1: The Risks of Unchecked Stubbornness

1. Ego-Driven Stubbornness: When Pride Takes Over

◈ **What It Looks Like:**

- Refusing to admit when you're wrong.
- Rejecting advice because it challenges your authority.
- Persisting in a failing plan out of fear of looking weak.

💡 **Example:**

- **Blockbuster's refusal to adapt to streaming was driven by overconfidence in their existing model.**

◈ **The Cost:**

- Missed opportunities for growth.
- Loss of trust from others.

◈ **Actionable Insight:**

✔ Regularly ask yourself: *"Am I being stubborn because I believe in this or because I don't want to admit I'm wrong?"*

2. The Isolation Trap: Alienating Others

◈ **What It Looks Like:**

- Insisting on doing everything your way.
- Ignoring team feedback or input.
- Dismissing collaboration as unnecessary.

💡 **Example:**

- **Leaders who micromanage or refuse to delegate often lose the support of their teams.**

◈ **The Cost:**

- Burnout from taking on too much alone.
- Loss of creativity and innovation from lack of collaboration.

◈ **Actionable Insight:**

✔ Involve others in decision-making to avoid isolating yourself.

✔ Ask for feedback and genuinely consider it.

3. Blind Persistence: Stuck in a Losing Strategy

◈ **What It Looks Like:**

- Doubling down on a failing idea instead of adapting.
- Ignoring clear evidence that it's time to pivot.

💡 **Example:**

- **Kodak's stubbornness about sticking to film photography, even as digital cameras rose, led to their decline.**

◈ **The Cost:**

- Wasted time, resources, and opportunities.

◈ **Actionable Insight:**

✔ Set measurable milestones to evaluate progress.

✔ Be willing to pivot if the data suggests it's necessary.

Phase 2: Recognizing When Stubbornness Is Working Against You

1. The Red Flags of Destructive Stubbornness

✔ You're constantly defending your decisions instead of explaining them.

✔ You reject advice without fully considering it.

✔ You feel stuck but refuse to change direction.

✔ Relationships or collaborations are suffering due to your inflexibility.

💡 **Actionable Exercise:**

✔ Create a "Stubbornness Checklist."

- Ask yourself: *"Is this helping me move forward, or am I stuck out of pride?"*

2. How to Differentiate Between Persistence and Stagnation

Persistence (Productive)	Stagnation (Destructive)
You're making measurable progress.	You're repeating the same actions with no results.
You're open to feedback while staying focused.	You dismiss all advice and input.
You're motivated by purpose.	You're motivated by fear of being wrong.

◈ **Lesson:** Recognize when your stubbornness is helping you push forward versus keeping you stuck.

3. The Role of Emotional Intelligence

✔ Emotional intelligence helps you recognize when your stubbornness is becoming counterproductive.

💡 **Key Questions to Ask Yourself:**

1️⃣ *"Am I listening to understand or just waiting to respond?"*

2️⃣ *"Am I prioritizing being right over being effective?"*

3️⃣ *"Am I open to learning something new from this situation?"*

Phase 3: Strategies to Avoid the Pitfalls of Stubbornness

1. Balance Confidence With Humility

✔ Confidence fuels your stubbornness, but humility keeps it in check.

💡 **How to Stay Balanced:**

1️⃣ Be confident in your vision but humble enough to admit mistakes.

2️⃣ View feedback as a tool for growth, not a threat to your authority.

🔷 **Example:**

- **Howard Schultz (Starbucks) balanced his confidence in his vision with openness to ideas from his team.**

2. Build a Trusted Feedback Circle

✔ Surround yourself with people who challenge your thinking and keep you grounded.

💡 **Actionable Tips:**

1️⃣ Identify 2–3 trusted advisors or team members.

2️⃣ Regularly seek their input on your decisions.

3️⃣ Actively listen and evaluate their advice.

◈ **Example:**

- **Bill Gates relied on his inner circle to refine Microsoft's strategy, even when it meant admitting he was wrong.**

3. Practice the "Pause and Reflect" Method

✔ Before making a decision, pause and reflect to avoid knee-jerk stubbornness.

💡 **Steps to Apply:**

1️⃣ Take a step back and assess the situation objectively.

2️⃣ Ask yourself: *"What's the best decision for the long term?"*

3️⃣ Sleep on major decisions to gain clarity.

Phase 4: Real-Life Stories of Overcoming the Dark Side of Stubbornness

1. Henry Ford: Learning From Feedback

- Ford's insistence on mass-producing the Model T nearly bankrupted his company when competitors offered more variety.
- He eventually pivoted, balancing his stubborn vision with customer demands.

💡 **Lesson:** Stubbornness must evolve with changing circumstances.

2. Oprah Winfrey: Listening to Her Team

- Oprah initially resisted advice to pivot her talk show's format but eventually adapted based on feedback, leading to her show's massive success.

💡 **Lesson:** Great leaders balance stubbornness with collaboration.

3. Airbnb: A Bold Pivot

- Airbnb founders stubbornly believed in their vision but adapted their approach when early strategies failed.
- They listened to feedback, refined their product, and became a global success.

💡 **Lesson:** Adaptation isn't abandoning your vision—it's refining it.

Phase 5: Exercises to Redirect Stubbornness Productively

1. The "Why Am I Stuck?" Journal

✔ Write down a situation where you feel stuck.

✔ Answer these questions:

- *"Am I resisting change out of fear or ego?"*
- *"What's one small step I can take to move forward?"*

2. The Feedback Challenge

✔ Seek feedback from 3 people on a current challenge.

✔ Write down their suggestions and commit to trying at least one of them.

3. The Humility Practice

✔ Once a week, admit a mistake or ask for help on something.

✔ Reflect on how it strengthens your leadership, not weakens it.

Conclusion: Embrace Stubbornness, But Stay Self-Aware

✔ **Stubbornness is a tool—it can build or break depending on how you use it.**

✔ **The key is to pair it with self-awareness, humility, and adaptability.**

💡 *"True strength lies in knowing when to stand firm and when to bend."*

🚀 **Next Chapter:** Becoming Unstoppable—How to Turn Stubbornness Into a Lifelong Strength.

CHAPTER 11

Becoming Unstoppable—How to Turn Stubbornness Into a Lifelong Strength

"Success is not final, failure is not fatal: It is the courage to continue that counts."

— Winston Churchill

Introduction: The Stubborn Mindset for Lifelong Growth

Stubbornness isn't just a short-term advantage—it's a trait that can make you **unstoppable throughout your life.**

✔ When paired with self-awareness and adaptability, stubbornness becomes a driving force for consistent growth.

✔ It gives you the persistence to overcome challenges, the resilience to bounce back from failure, and the courage to pursue your goals relentlessly.

💡 **Becoming unstoppable doesn't mean never facing obstacles—it means refusing to let them stop you.**

In this final chapter, we'll explore:

1. How to integrate purposeful stubbornness into every aspect of your life.
2. Daily practices that reinforce resilience, growth, and determination.
3. How to cultivate a legacy of stubborn success.

Phase 1: Building an Unstoppable Foundation

1. Align Your Stubbornness With Your Core Values

◈ **Why It Matters:**

- Stubbornness becomes destructive when it's misaligned with what truly matters to you.
- Aligning it with your core values ensures that your persistence is always purposeful.

💡 **Example:**

- **Mahatma Gandhi's stubbornness was rooted in his unwavering belief in nonviolence and justice.**

◈ **Actionable Insight:**

✔ Write down your top 3 core values.

✔ Ask yourself: *"Is my stubbornness helping me live out these values?"*

2. Adopt a Long-Term Perspective

◈ **The Mindset Shift:**

- Stubborn people focus on the long game, not immediate results.
- They understand that success is a marathon, not a sprint.

💡 **Example:**

- **Jeff Bezos started Amazon with a 10-year vision, enduring years of low profits before the company became a global powerhouse.**

◈ **Actionable Insight:**

✔ Set long-term goals and break them into manageable milestones.

✔ Ask yourself: *"How will this decision affect my goals 5, 10, or 20 years from now?"*

3. Build Emotional and Mental Resilience

◈ **Why It's Crucial:**

- Stubbornness without resilience can lead to burnout.
- Emotional strength ensures you can keep going even when the road gets tough.

💡 **How to Build Resilience:**

✔ Practice mindfulness to manage stress.

✔ Reframe challenges as opportunities for growth.

✔ Surround yourself with supportive, like-minded individuals.

Phase 2: Daily Habits to Reinforce Your Stubborn Strength

1. Start Every Day With Intention

✔ A clear morning routine sets the tone for a productive day.

💡 **Example:**

- **Oprah Winfrey begins her day with meditation and gratitude, grounding herself in purpose.**

◈ **Action Step:**

✔ Spend 5 minutes each morning visualizing your goals and planning your day with intention.

2. Practice Consistency Over Perfection

✔ Success comes from showing up daily, even when you're not at your best.

💡 **Example:**

- **Stephen King writes every day, even on holidays, keeping his creative momentum alive.**

◈ **Action Step:**

✔ Choose one habit aligned with your goal and commit to it daily, no matter what.

3. Reflect and Refine

✔ Regular self-reflection helps you identify what's working and where you can improve.

💡 **Example:**

- **Elon Musk constantly evaluates his companies' progress, adjusting strategies as needed.**

◆ **Action Step:**

✔ End each day by reflecting on:

- What went well?
- What didn't?
- What can I improve tomorrow?

Phase 3: Cultivating an Unstoppable Legacy

1. Pass on Your Stubborn Strength

✔ True success is about inspiring others to persist and achieve their goals.

💡 **Example:**

- **Serena Williams mentors young athletes, teaching them the value of resilience and determination.**

◆ **Actionable Insight:**

✔ Share your story and lessons with others to inspire persistence.

2. Leave a Lasting Impact

✔ Use your stubbornness to create something that endures beyond your lifetime.

💡 **Example:**

- **Walt Disney's vision for creativity and imagination lives on through his company and theme parks.**

◆ **Action Step:**

✔ Ask yourself: *"What legacy do I want to leave behind?"*

Phase 4: Exercises to Become Unstoppable

1. The Resilience Tracker

✔ Write down challenges you faced this week.

✔ Note how you overcame them and what you learned.

💡 **Lesson:** Tracking your resilience builds confidence in your ability to persist.

2. The Vision Roadmap

✔ Create a roadmap for your long-term vision.

✔ Break it into yearly, monthly, and weekly goals.

💡 **Lesson:** A clear plan keeps your stubbornness focused and productive.

3. The Gratitude + Grit Journal

✔ Each day, write down:

- 3 things you're grateful for.
- 1 challenge you overcame.

💡 **Lesson:** Gratitude reinforces positivity, while grit reminds you of your strength.

Conclusion: Turning Stubbornness Into a Lifelong Superpower

✔ **Stubbornness is not just about persistence—it's about purpose, resilience, and impact.**

✔ **When used wisely, it becomes a lifelong strength that fuels success and inspires others.**

💡 *"The unstoppable aren't those who never fall—they're the ones who rise every time they do."*

🚀 **Final Note:** Your stubbornness is your superpower—use it to chase your dreams, overcome challenges, and leave a lasting legacy.

CHAPTER 12

The Science of Mental Toughness—How to Build an Unbreakable Mindset

> **"The moment you accept total responsibility for everything in your life is the moment you claim the power to change anything in your life."**
>
> — Hal Elrod

Introduction: Why Mental Toughness Matters

The ability to push through challenges, setbacks, and failures without breaking is what separates those who succeed from those who quit.

✔ Mental toughness is **not** about never feeling stress, doubt, or pain—it's about refusing to let those emotions stop you.

✔ It is **not** something you're born with—it's something you develop.

✔ It is **not** about talent—it's about resilience, discipline, and a refusal to quit.

💡 **This chapter will show you how to train your mind to become unbreakable, so no obstacle, rejection, or failure can hold you back.**

Phase 1: Understanding Mental Toughness

1. What Is Mental Toughness?

◈ **Mental toughness is the ability to stay focused, determined, and resilient despite obstacles.**

✔ It allows you to keep moving forward when everything in you wants to stop.

✔ It enables you to endure discomfort, push through fear, and rise after failure.

✔ It's the key to long-term success in business, sports, relationships, and personal growth.

💡 **Example:**

- **Michael Jordan was cut from his high school basketball team.** Instead of quitting, he trained harder and became one of the greatest athletes in history.

◈ **Lesson: Mentally tough people don't quit—they adjust, adapt, and keep going.**

2. The Science Behind Mental Toughness

🔬 **What Research Says About Grit and Resilience:**

- Angela Duckworth's research on *grit* found that **passion + perseverance = success.**
- Studies on elite athletes show that **mental resilience is more important than physical ability.**
- Neuroscience reveals that **mentally tough people have stronger prefrontal cortex activity, which helps them regulate emotions and resist impulses.**

💡 **Key Takeaway:**

✔ Mental toughness is like a muscle—the more you train it, the stronger it gets.

3. The Core Pillars of Mental Toughness

1️⃣ **Emotional Control** – The ability to manage stress, fear, and frustration without losing focus.

2️⃣ **Resilience** – The ability to bounce back quickly from failure.

3️⃣ **Discipline** – The ability to stick to your commitments, even when motivation fades.

4️⃣ **Adaptability** – The ability to adjust to challenges and find solutions instead of excuses.

💡 **Example:**

- **Navy SEALs are trained to control their emotions under extreme pressure, helping them make critical decisions in life-or-death situations.**

◈ **Lesson: Building these four pillars will make you mentally unstoppable.**

Phase 2: Training Yourself for Mental Toughness

1. The "No Excuses" Mindset

✔ Excuses are the #1 killer of mental toughness.

💡 **Common Excuses vs. The Mentally Tough Response:**

Excuse	Mentally Tough Response
"I'm too tired."	"I'll do it tired."
"I don't feel like it."	"My feelings don't decide my actions."
"It's too hard."	"Good—challenges make me stronger."
"I don't have time."	"I make time for what matters."

◆ **Action Step:**

✔ The next time you catch yourself making an excuse, reframe it into a **mentally tough response.**

2. The Power of Exposure Therapy

✔ **The more you face discomfort, the less control it has over you.**

💡 **Example:**

- **Public speakers who repeatedly put themselves in uncomfortable situations (small speeches, interviews, live videos) become immune to stage fright over time.**

◆ **Action Step:**

✔ Identify something that makes you uncomfortable and **gradually expose yourself to it.**

✔ Increase the difficulty step by step until it no longer bothers you.

3. How to Rewire Your Brain for Resilience

✔ Your brain **naturally** wants to avoid pain and discomfort. But you can train it to push through obstacles.

💡 **Exercise: The "Reframing Challenges" Technique**

1️⃣ Write down your biggest current challenge.

2️⃣ Next to it, write **one hidden advantage** this challenge gives you.

3️⃣ Repeat this daily to rewire your brain to **see problems as opportunities.**

Phase 3: Developing Daily Mental Toughness Habits

1. The Cold Shower Challenge

✔ Taking cold showers trains your mind to **tolerate discomfort.**

✔ It strengthens willpower, improves discipline, and increases stress resilience.

💡 **Action Step:**

✔ Take a **30-second cold shower** every morning.

✔ Increase the duration over time to push your mental limits.

2. The "Do It Anyway" Rule

✔ **Discipline beats motivation.**

✔ Mentally tough people **act even when they don't feel like it.**

💡 **Example:**

- **Jocko Willink, former Navy SEAL, wakes up at 4:30 AM daily to train—no excuses.**

◈ **Action Step:**

✔ Identify one habit (exercise, writing, learning) and commit to doing it daily, **no matter how you feel.**

3. The "One More Rep" Technique

✔ Train yourself to **always push beyond your perceived limits.**

💡 **Example:**

- If you plan to do 20 push-ups, do **one more.**
- If you commit to writing for 30 minutes, go **five more minutes.**

◈ **Lesson:** This habit **rewires your brain to stop quitting at the first sign of fatigue.**

Phase 4: Stories of Mental Toughness in Action

1. David Goggins: The Toughest Man Alive

- Goggins went from overweight and depressed to a Navy SEAL, ultramarathon runner, and elite endurance athlete.
- His motto? **"Stay hard."**
- He trains his mind by **seeking discomfort daily.**

💡 **Lesson: If you stop making excuses, your potential is limitless.**

2. Elon Musk: Mental Resilience in Business

- Musk nearly lost Tesla and SpaceX but refused to quit.
- He **worked 100-hour weeks** and invested every dollar to keep his vision alive.

💡 **Lesson: Mental toughness is essential for long-term success.**

3. Bethany Hamilton: The Surfer Who Refused to Quit

- Bethany lost her arm in a shark attack but stubbornly returned to professional surfing.

- She learned to re-balance and compete at the highest level despite her injury.

💡 **Lesson: Challenges don't define you—your response to them does.**

Phase 5: Exercises to Strengthen Mental Toughness

1. The 30-Day Mental Toughness Challenge

✔ **Week 1:** Wake up 30 minutes earlier than usual.

✔ **Week 2:** Do one thing that makes you uncomfortable daily.

✔ **Week 3:** Push beyond your limits in one area (work, fitness, learning).

✔ **Week 4:** Go one full day without complaining.

2. The "Hardest Task First" Rule

✔ Each day, **start with the most difficult task** instead of procrastinating.

✔ This builds willpower and mental strength.

3. The Visualization Ritual

✔ Every morning, **visualize yourself succeeding in the face of challenges.**

✔ This conditions your mind to expect resilience, not fear.

Conclusion: Your Mind Is Your Strongest Weapon

✔ **Mental toughness is not about being fearless—it's about acting despite fear.**

✔ **You don't need to be born strong—you can train your mind to be unstoppable.**

💡 *"Your mind will quit long before your body does. Train it to push forward."*

🚀 **Next Chapter:** Emotional Stubbornness—Controlling Your Feelings Instead of Being Controlled by Them.

CHAPTER 13

Emotional Stubbornness—Controlling Your Feelings Instead of Being Controlled by Them

"You have power over your mind—not outside events. Realize this, and you will find strength."

— Marcus Aurelius

Introduction: Why Emotional Stubbornness Is a Superpower

Most people **let their emotions dictate their actions**—but the strongest individuals **control their emotions** instead of letting their emotions control them.

✔ Emotional stubbornness isn't about suppressing feelings—it's about mastering them.

✔ It means staying **calm under pressure, making rational decisions, and refusing to be emotionally manipulated.**

✔ It is the ability to **stay strong in the face of criticism, failure, and emotional turbulence.**

💡 **This chapter will teach you how to take full control of your emotions and use emotional stubbornness as a strength instead of a weakness.**

Phase 1: Understanding Emotional Stubbornness

1. What Is Emotional Stubbornness?

◈ **Emotional stubbornness is the ability to remain emotionally steady, no matter the circumstances.**

✔ It helps you **stay calm under stress.**

✔ It prevents others from **manipulating you emotionally.**

✔ It allows you to **make clear, rational decisions instead of impulsive ones.**

💡 **Example:**

- **Stoic philosophers like Marcus Aurelius trained themselves to remain emotionally unaffected by external events, making them unshakable leaders.**

◈ **Lesson: Control your emotions, or your emotions will control you.**

2. Why Most People Are Emotionally Weak

✔ They **react emotionally** instead of thinking logically.

✔ They let criticism **destroy their confidence.**

✔ They allow rejection **to dictate their self-worth.**

✔ They fear **discomfort and seek constant validation.**

💡 **Example:**

- **An emotionally weak person takes every negative comment personally, while an emotionally stubborn person ignores it and focuses on self-improvement.**

◈ **Lesson: Emotional toughness is a skill you must develop through training.**

3. The Science of Emotional Control

🔬 **What Research Shows About Emotion Regulation:**

✔ Studies show that **emotionally resilient people activate their prefrontal cortex more than their amygdala** (the brain's emotional center).

✔ This allows them to **stay logical even under stress** while others react impulsively.

✔ Mental toughness training (such as mindfulness) **rewires the brain to resist emotional overreactions.**

💡 **Key Takeaway:**

✔ **You can train your brain to handle stress, rejection, and criticism better.**

Phase 2: Training Yourself for Emotional Stubbornness

1. The "Pause Before Reacting" Rule

✔ Instead of reacting emotionally, **pause, breathe, and think.**

✔ This prevents emotional outbursts and **allows logical thinking to take over.**

💡 **Example:**

- **A top CEO never reacts immediately to criticism—he takes time to process it before responding calmly.**

🔶 **Action Step:**

✔ When faced with an emotionally charged situation, **take a deep breath and count to five before responding.**

2. The Power of Neutral Thinking

✔ Instead of seeing situations as **good or bad, train yourself to see them as neutral.**

✔ Neutral thinking **removes emotional bias and helps you make smarter choices.**

💡 **Example:**

- **Michael Jordan didn't celebrate victories or dwell on losses—he stayed focused on what's next.**

◈ **Action Step:**

✔ Practice saying, **"It is what it is. Now, what's next?"**

3. How to Build Emotional Detachment

✔ Emotionally stubborn people **don't take things personally.**

✔ They separate **facts from feelings** to avoid unnecessary stress.

💡 **Exercise: The "Step Outside Yourself" Technique**

1️⃣ Imagine you are watching yourself from a third-person perspective.

2️⃣ Ask, *"If this were happening to a friend, what advice would I give them?"*

3️⃣ Follow that advice instead of reacting emotionally.

Phase 3: How to Handle Emotional Manipulation

1. Recognizing Emotional Triggers

✔ **Manipulators use emotions to control you.**

✔ If they can make you **angry, insecure, or doubtful**, they can **influence your decisions.**

💡 **Example:**

- **Toxic people often guilt-trip others to get their way.** Emotionally stubborn individuals recognize this and refuse to play into their hands.

◈ **Action Step:**

✔ Identify your biggest emotional triggers and **train yourself to stay calm when faced with them.**

2. How to Avoid Emotional Blackmail

✔ Some people will try to **guilt-trip, shame, or emotionally manipulate you** into doing things.

✔ Emotionally stubborn people **set clear boundaries** and refuse to be controlled by guilt.

💡 **Example:**

- **Warren Buffett never lets emotions cloud his business decisions.** He operates based on logic, not pressure from others.

◈ **Action Step:**

✔ Practice saying **"No" without explaining or justifying yourself.**

Phase 4: Emotional Stubbornness in the Face of Criticism & Rejection

1. How to Handle Criticism Without Letting It Crush You

✔ Most people take criticism **personally** and let it damage their confidence.

✔ Stubborn achievers **analyze criticism rationally** and use it for self-improvement.

💡 **Example:**

- **J.K. Rowling was rejected by 12 publishers, but she didn't let it destroy her confidence—she stayed stubborn and kept submitting.**

◈ **Action Step:**

✔ When criticized, ask yourself:

- *"Is this true?"* (If yes, improve.)
- *"Is this nonsense?"* (If yes, ignore.)

2. Turning Rejection Into Strength

✔ Rejection is an **opinion, not a fact.**

✔ Emotionally stubborn people **don't let rejection affect their self-worth.**

💡 **Example:**

- **Oprah Winfrey was fired from her first TV job and told she wasn't fit for television.** She refused to accept that opinion and became a billionaire media mogul.

◈ **Action Step:**

✔ Each time you face rejection, remind yourself:

- *"This is just one person's opinion. It does not define me."*

3. The "Emotional Armor" Technique

✔ Train yourself to be **mentally and emotionally untouchable.**

💡 **How to Build Your Emotional Armor:**

1 **Detach from opinions.** What others say doesn't define you.

2 **See rejection as redirection.**

3 **Focus on your own validation, not external approval.**

Phase 5: Exercises to Master Emotional Stubbornness

1. The "Discomfort Training" Challenge

✔ Expose yourself to **emotionally difficult situations** on purpose.

💡 **Example Exercises:**

✔ Say "No" to something you normally say "Yes" to out of guilt.

✔ Go a full day without reacting to negativity.

2. The "Reframing Negativity" Exercise

✔ When something negative happens, **force yourself to find one positive lesson.**

✔ Do this **daily** to train your brain to focus on solutions, not problems.

3. The "No Reaction" Test

✔ Go one full day without reacting emotionally to **anything.**

✔ No frustration, no irritation—just **calm control.**

💡 **Lesson: The less you react emotionally, the more power you gain.**

Conclusion: Master Your Emotions, Master Your Life

✔ **Emotional stubbornness is not about suppressing emotions—it's about controlling them.**

✔ **It's about making decisions based on logic, not impulses.**

✔ **When you control your emotions, no one can control you.**

💡 *"Strong minds control emotions. Weak minds are controlled by them."*

🚀 **Next Chapter:** How to Stay Stubborn When Everyone Else Quits.

CHAPTER 14

How to Stay Stubborn When Everyone Else Quits

"Most people give up just when they're about to achieve success. They quit on the one-yard line."

— Ross Perot

Introduction: Why People Quit Too Soon

Most people quit **not because they can't succeed, but because they lose patience, motivation, or belief in themselves.**

✔ The **biggest difference** between those who succeed and those who fail is **stubborn consistency.**

✔ Stubborn achievers don't quit **when things get hard—they double down and push through.**

✔ Quitting is a habit, and so is refusing to quit.

💡 **This chapter will teach you how to keep going when everyone else gives up—so you can achieve what others only dream of.**

Phase 1: The Real Reasons People Quit

1. The 5 Main Reasons People Give Up

Most people quit because they:

❌ **Expect results too quickly** – If success doesn't happen fast, they assume it's impossible.

❌ **Let fear of failure stop them** – They'd rather quit than risk looking bad.

❌ **Lack discipline** – They rely on motivation instead of routine.

❌ **Lose belief in themselves** – They let doubt creep in.

❌ **Listen to negative opinions** – They care too much about what others think.

💡 **Example:**

- **J.K. Rowling's first Harry Potter book was rejected by 12 publishers. If she had quit at rejection #5 or #10, she would have never become the best-selling author of all time.**

🔶 **Lesson: Most people quit when they are just one step away from success. Don't be most people.**

2. Why Stubborn Achievers Never Give Up

✔ They understand that **success is not about intensity, but consistency.**

✔ They know that **overnight success is a myth—real success takes years of effort.**

✔ They focus on **progress, not perfection.**

💡 **Example:**

- **Colonel Sanders started KFC in his 60s after 1,009 rejections. Most people would have quit after 10.**

◈ **Lesson: Success is not about how fast you get there—it's about refusing to stop.**

Phase 2: How to Stay Stubborn When Things Get Hard

1. Rewire Your Brain to See Obstacles as Challenges

✔ Mentally tough people don't see challenges as reasons to quit.

✔ They **train their brain** to see obstacles as **signs they are on the right path.**

💡 **Example:**

- **Elon Musk faced multiple near-bankruptcies with Tesla and SpaceX, but instead of quitting, he pushed forward—and turned them into billion-dollar companies.**

◈ **Action Step:**

✔ The next time you face a challenge, tell yourself:

- *"This isn't a sign to stop—it's a test to see if I'm worthy of success."*

2. Master the "Last Man Standing" Strategy

✔ **Most people quit when things get uncomfortable.**

✔ If you simply **outlast everyone else, you win by default.**

💡 **Example:**

- **Jeff Bezos outlasted all his early competitors when Amazon was struggling. Today, it's a trillion-dollar company.**

◈ **Action Step:**

✔ Remind yourself daily: *"If I just keep going, I'll outlast everyone who quits."*

3. Find Fuel in Failure

✔ Mentally tough people **don't fear failure—they use it as motivation.**

✔ **Every failure is proof you are making progress.**

💡 **Example:**

- **Thomas Edison didn't see 1,000 failed lightbulb attempts as failures—he saw them as 1,000 steps toward success.**

◈ **Action Step:**

✔ After every failure, ask: *"What did I learn, and how does this get me closer to success?"*

Phase 3: Stubborn Routines That Keep You Going

1. The "No Matter What" Rule

✔ Choose one **daily habit** that brings you closer to your goal.

✔ Do it **no matter what**—even on bad days.

💡 **Example:**

- **Stephen King writes 1,000 words every single day, no exceptions.**

◈ **Action Step:**

✔ Pick a non-negotiable habit (workout, writing, studying) and commit to it daily.

2. The 5-Year Rule

✔ Most people quit after a few weeks or months.

✔ **Decide upfront that you will stick with your goal for at least five years.**

💡 **Example:**

- **Walt Disney spent years facing rejection before launching Disney Studios.**

◈ **Action Step:**

✔ Write this down: *"I will commit to my goal for the next five years, no matter what."*

3. The "Remember Why You Started" Technique

✔ When you feel like quitting, reconnect with your **original motivation.**

✔ The bigger your "why," the stronger your perseverance.

💡 **Example:**

- **Arnold Schwarzenegger stayed committed to bodybuilding for years because he was obsessed with his vision of success.**

◈ **Action Step:**

✔ Write your goal on paper and read it every morning to keep it alive.

Phase 4: When People Doubt You—Use It as Fuel

1. How to Handle Critics and Naysayers

✔ People will tell you to quit.

✔ Most of them quit on their own dreams, and they want you to do the same.

💡 **Example:**

- **Oprah was told she wasn't fit for TV—imagine if she had listened!**

◈ **Action Step:**

✔ The next time someone doubts you, think:

- *"They don't see my vision, but I do."*

2. Stop Seeking Permission to Keep Going

✔ The biggest mistake people make is **waiting for approval from others.**

✔ Stubborn achievers don't need permission—they keep going regardless.

💡 **Example:**

- **Elon Musk didn't wait for approval before launching SpaceX. He just did it.**

◈ **Action Step:**

✔ Stop explaining yourself. Take action and let success speak for itself.

Phase 5: Exercises to Strengthen Your Stubbornness

1. The 30-Day No Quit Challenge

✔ Pick one habit related to your goal.

✔ Do it every single day for 30 days, no matter what.

💡 **Lesson: If you can commit for 30 days, you can commit for life.**

2. The "What If I Don't Quit?" Exercise

✔ Ask yourself:

- *"What happens if I keep going for 5 more years?"*
- *"How much progress can I make if I never stop?"*

💡 **Lesson: Most people underestimate what they can achieve with stubborn consistency.**

3. The 10-Year Letter

✔ Write a letter to yourself, 10 years in the future.

✔ Describe what your life looks like **if you refuse to quit.**

💡 **Lesson: The best version of you is waiting on the other side of persistence.**

Conclusion: The Power of Being the Last One Standing

✔ **Most people quit—but you don't have to.**

✔ **Success is about sticking around longer than anyone else.**

✔ **The longer you hold on, the higher your chances of winning.**

💡 *"Great things take time. The only way to fail is to quit."*

🚀 **Next Chapter:** Overcoming Self-Doubt—Being Stubborn About Your Potential.

CHAPTER 15

Overcoming Self-Doubt—Being Stubborn About Your Potential

"Doubt kills more dreams than failure ever will."

— Suzy Kassem

Introduction: Why Self-Doubt Destroys More Dreams Than Failure

Most people fail **not because they aren't talented, smart, or capable—but because they don't believe they are.**

✔ **Self-doubt is the biggest enemy of success.**

✔ **People quit, hesitate, or play small—not because they can't, but because they think they can't.**

✔ **The most stubborn people refuse to doubt themselves, even when the world does.**

💡 **This chapter will teach you how to destroy self-doubt and become stubborn about your own potential.**

Phase 1: Understanding Self-Doubt and Where It Comes From

1. Why Do We Doubt Ourselves?

✔ **Self-doubt is not natural—it's learned.**

✔ We are conditioned from childhood to **seek approval** and fear making mistakes.

💡 **Common Sources of Self-Doubt:**

1️⃣ **Negative past experiences** – Failures make us fear future risks.

2️⃣ **Comparison syndrome** – Seeing others succeed makes us feel behind.

3️⃣ **Fear of judgment** – Worrying about what others think holds us back.

4️⃣ **Perfectionism** – If we're not perfect, we think we're not good enough.

💠 **Lesson: Self-doubt isn't real—it's a mental habit you can break.**

2. The Difference Between Self-Doubt and Self-Awareness

✔ **Self-awareness is knowing your strengths and weaknesses.**

✔ **Self-doubt is assuming your weaknesses define you.**

💡 **Example:**

- A confident person **acknowledges** their flaws but still believes in themselves.
- A doubtful person **obsesses** over their flaws and lets them stop them.

💠 **Lesson: You don't need to be perfect—you just need to believe you can improve.**

3. The "What If" Trap—How Doubt Paralyzes People

✔ Most people quit because they ask themselves negative "what if" questions:

✕ *"What if I fail?"*

✕ *"What if people laugh at me?"*

✕ *"What if I'm not good enough?"*

💡 **Action Step:**

✔ Flip the question to a **positive** "what if":

☑ *"What if I succeed?"*

☑ *"What if this changes my life?"*

☑ *"What if I'm capable of more than I think?"*

Phase 2: How to Kill Self-Doubt and Build Unshakable Self-Belief

1. Train Your Brain to Trust Yourself

✔ The **more you prove to yourself that you can take action, the less you doubt yourself.**

✔ Confidence isn't something you're born with—it's something you build.

💡 **Example:**

- **Will Smith said confidence comes from doing hard things repeatedly until they feel easy.**

◈ **Action Step:**

✔ Do **one small thing daily** that proves you can follow through. (Even if it's just making your bed, working out, or finishing a task.)

2. Rewrite Your Mental Script

✔ Most people live by a **negative mental script** they don't even realize is playing.

✔ You must replace it with a **stubbornly positive internal voice.**

💡 **Exercise: "The Self-Talk Rewrite"**

1️⃣ Write down 5 negative things you tell yourself.

2️⃣ Rewrite them into **empowering** statements.

3️⃣ Repeat them every morning.

◈ **Example:**

❌ "I'm not smart enough." → ✅ "I can figure anything out if I work hard enough."

❌ "I always mess things up." → ✅ "Every mistake makes me better."

3. Stop Looking for Approval—Validate Yourself

✔ **The strongest people don't wait for permission to believe in themselves.**

✔ You don't need anyone's approval to chase your goals.

💡 **Example:**

- **Oprah Winfrey was told she wasn't fit for television. If she had waited for approval, she would have never succeeded.**

◈ **Action Step:**

✔ **Stop asking, "Am I good enough?" and start asking, "How can I get better?"**

Phase 3: Building Stubborn Confidence—Even When Others Doubt You

1. How to Handle People Who Doubt You

✔ Not everyone will believe in you—but that's their problem, not yours.

💡 **Example:**

- **Elon Musk was told Tesla and SpaceX would fail. He ignored the doubters and kept going.**

◈ **Action Step:**

✔ The next time someone doubts you, think:

- *"They don't see my vision, but I do."*

2. The "Past Proof" Method—Using Your Own Success as Evidence

✔ You've already overcome things that once seemed impossible.

✔ Use your past wins to remind yourself that you can do hard things.

💡 **Example:**

- **Every successful athlete, entrepreneur, and artist was once a beginner.**

◈ **Action Step:**

✔ Write down **5 challenges you've already overcome** in life.

✔ Look at this list whenever doubt creeps in.

3. Get Addicted to Small Wins

✔ The more **small wins** you collect, the more confidence you build.

✔ This makes doubt disappear over time.

💡 **Example:**

- **Kobe Bryant built his confidence by outworking everyone—he knew no one could out-train him.**

◈ **Action Step:**

✔ Set **one small daily goal** and complete it, no matter what.

Phase 4: When Self-Doubt Hits—How to Push Through

1. The "Just One More" Rule

✔ When you feel like quitting, **do just one more.**

💡 **Example:**

- If you're exhausted at the gym, do **one more rep.**
- If you're doubting your project, **work for 5 more minutes.**

◈ **Lesson: Momentum kills doubt. The more you push, the more confidence you build.**

2. The "Act First, Think Later" Technique

✔ Overthinking fuels doubt. The best way to kill doubt? **Take action before you feel ready.**

💡 **Example:**

- **Most people wait until they feel confident to act—stubborn achievers act until they feel confident.**

◈ **Action Step:**

✔ Commit to **taking action before you feel ready.**

3. The "If Not Me, Then Who?" Mindset

✔ **Every successful person was once an ordinary person—until they decided to believe in themselves.**

💡 **Example:**

- **Every champion, millionaire, and icon was once a beginner.**

◈ **Action Step:**

✔ Ask yourself: *"If they could do it, why can't I?"*

Phase 5: Exercises to Permanently Kill Self-Doubt

1. The "Confidence Bank" Exercise

✔ Write down **one small win every day.**

✔ Over time, you'll build an unshakable belief in yourself.

💡 **Lesson: Confidence is built, not given.**

2. The "Fear List" Challenge

✔ Write down **3 things you avoid because of self-doubt.**

✔ Do one of them this week.

💡 **Lesson: Every time you face fear, you weaken self-doubt.**

3. The "Failure is Feedback" Mindset Shift

✔ Write down **a failure you're afraid of.**

✔ Next to it, write **one way failure could help you grow.**

💡 **Lesson: Doubt fades when you stop fearing failure.**

Conclusion: Stubborn People Refuse to Doubt Themselves

✔ **If you refuse to doubt yourself, you'll go further than 99% of people.**

✔ **The only difference between winners and quitters is belief.**

✔ **Success is just stubborn self-belief applied over time.**

💡 *"You either believe in yourself, or you let the world decide your worth."*

🚀 **Next Chapter:** The Art of Stubborn Negotiation—How to Win Without Being Overbearing.

CHAPTER 16

The Art of Stubborn Negotiation—How to Win Without Being Overbearing

> **"You don't get what you deserve, you get what you negotiate."**
>
> — Chester L. Karrass

Introduction: Why Negotiation is a Stubborn Person's Superpower

Negotiation isn't just for business deals—it's a **daily skill** that can help you:

✔ Get a **higher salary.**

✔ Convince people to see your point of view.

✔ Win better deals in business, sales, and even personal relationships.

Most people struggle with negotiation because they fear rejection, compromise too easily, or feel uncomfortable demanding what they deserve.

💡 **This chapter will teach you how to use stubbornness to negotiate powerfully—without being aggressive or manipulative.**

Phase 1: The Stubborn Negotiator's Mindset

1. Why Most People Fail at Negotiation

✔ **They ask instead of assert.**

✔ **They accept the first offer out of fear of rejection.**

✔ **They compromise too quickly to avoid conflict.**

✔ **They don't realize that everything is negotiable.**

💡 **Example:**

- **Most employees accept their first salary offer instead of negotiating—costing them thousands of dollars over time.**

◈ **Lesson: The best negotiators aren't aggressive—they're confidently stubborn.**

2. The Stubborn Negotiator's Core Beliefs

✔ **Everything is negotiable.** (If you never ask, the answer is always no.)

✔ **Silence is power.** (The less you talk, the more control you have.)

✔ **The first offer is never the best offer.** (Always counter.)

✔ **Confidence is non-verbal.** (How you say things matters more than what you say.)

💡 **Example:**

- **Jeff Bezos built Amazon by stubbornly negotiating better deals with suppliers—never taking the first price.**

◈ **Lesson: Negotiation isn't about arguing—it's about knowing your worth and standing firm.**

Phase 2: How to Negotiate Without Being Pushy

1. The "Calm Stubbornness" Technique

✔ The best negotiators are **firm but polite.**

✔ They use **calm confidence** to make the other person respect them.

💡 **Example:**

- **Warren Buffett is known for negotiating billion-dollar deals while staying calm and never raising his voice.**

◈ **Action Step:**

✔ Practice saying:

- *"I understand where you're coming from, but I can't accept that."*

2. The Power of Silence—How to Make People Give You More

✔ **When you make an offer, stop talking.**

✔ Most people hate awkward silence and will offer something better just to fill the gap.

💡 **Example:**

- **In sales, the person who speaks first after an offer usually loses.**

◈ **Action Step:**

✔ The next time someone gives you an offer, **pause for 10 seconds before responding.**

3. Always Have a Backup Plan (BATNA Strategy)

✔ **BATNA = Best Alternative to a Negotiated Agreement.**

✔ If you walk into a negotiation with **other options**, you have more power.

💡 **Example:**

- **When negotiating a job offer, having multiple offers makes you more valuable.**

◈ **Action Step:**

✔ Always have **another option ready** before negotiating anything.

Phase 3: Stubborn Negotiation Strategies That Work Every Time

1. The "Anchoring" Trick—Set the First Number

✔ **Whoever gives the first number controls the negotiation.**

✔ If you aim high, the final deal will be closer to what you want.

💡 **Example:**

- **Real estate agents set higher initial prices so buyers feel like they're getting a deal when negotiating down.**

◈ **Action Step:**

✔ **Always be the first to set the number**—make the other person react to your offer.

2. The "If-Then" Technique—Creating Win-Win Deals

✔ People are more likely to agree when they see a **mutual benefit.**

💡 **Example Phrases:**

- *"If I agree to this price, then I need a longer warranty."*
- *"If you can increase my salary, then I'll take on more responsibilities."*

◈ **Action Step:**

✔ **Always attach a condition to your agreement.**

3. The "Take It or Leave It" Confidence Move

✔ Sometimes, the best move is to **be willing to walk away.**

✔ This shows the other person that you **can't be pressured.**

💡 **Example:**

- **Steve Jobs was infamous for walking away from bad deals—forcing others to meet his terms.**

◈ **Action Step:**

✔ **Know your limits—and be ready to walk away if they're not met.**

Phase 4: Real-World Negotiation Scenarios & How to Win Them

1. How to Negotiate a Higher Salary

✔ **Research the market rate** before your interview.

✔ **Let them make the first offer, then counter.**

✔ Use the phrase: *"Is that the best you can do?"*

💡 **Example:**

- **People who negotiate their salaries earn 10-20% more over their careers.**

◈ **Action Step:**

✔ Before your next job offer, practice saying:

- *"I was expecting something in the range of X."*

2. How to Negotiate Better Prices in Business or Sales

✔ Always ask for a **bulk discount or lower rate.**

✔ Use silence after asking for a better deal.

✔ If they say no, ask: *"What can you do instead?"*

💡 **Example:**

- **Big companies negotiate lower prices on everything—because they ask.**

◈ **Action Step:**

✔ The next time you make a big purchase, **ask for a discount.**

3. How to Negotiate in Personal Relationships

✔ Negotiation isn't just about money—it's about getting what you want in relationships, too.

✔ **Don't argue—frame your request as a win-win.**

💡 **Example:**

- Instead of saying:

✘ *"You never help with housework."*

☑ Try: *"If we split chores, we'll both have more free time."*

◈ **Action Step:**

✔ Use the **"If-Then" technique** in personal conversations.

Phase 5: Exercises to Become a Stubborn Negotiator

1. The "Low-Stakes Negotiation" Challenge

✔ Start negotiating small things—coffee, bills, rent—just to practice.

✔ The more you do it, the easier it becomes.

💡 **Lesson: Negotiation is a skill—you get better by using it.**

2. The "Pause Before You Answer" Drill

✔ Practice **waiting 5 seconds before responding** in conversations.

✔ This helps you get comfortable with silence, which gives you power.

💡 **Lesson: Patience makes you a better negotiator.**

3. The "Set Your Number First" Game

✔ Pick any upcoming negotiation (salary, contract, purchase).

✔ Practice stating **your number first** and anchoring the conversation.

💡 **Lesson: The one who sets the first number controls the deal.**

Conclusion: The Stubborn Negotiator Always Wins

✔ **Negotiation isn't about aggression—it's about confidence and persistence.**

✔ **The strongest negotiators don't push—they hold firm.**

✔ **If you don't negotiate, you're leaving money and opportunities on the table.**

💡 *"You don't get what you deserve. You get what you negotiate."*

🚀 **Next Chapter:** Stubbornness in Love—When to Hold On and When to Let Go.

CHAPTER 17

Stubbornness in Love—When to Hold On and When to Let Go

"A strong relationship requires choosing each other even when it's difficult."

— Unknown

Introduction: The Role of Stubbornness in Love

Love is complicated, and stubbornness can be both a **relationship strength** and a **destructive force.**

✔ **Sometimes, stubborn love means fighting for someone even when things get tough.**

✔ **Other times, it means knowing when to walk away from something that no longer serves you.**

The key? Knowing when to hold on and when to let go.

💡 **This chapter will help you use stubbornness wisely in love—to build strong, lasting relationships without letting pride, ego, or toxicity ruin them.**

Phase 1: The Right Kind of Stubbornness in Relationships

1. The Difference Between Healthy and Toxic Stubbornness

✔ **Healthy stubbornness in love means:**

- Fighting for the relationship, even through tough times.
- Being committed to growth, compromise, and mutual respect.

✖ **Toxic stubbornness in love means:**

- Refusing to admit mistakes or take responsibility.
- Holding on to a relationship that is no longer healthy.

💡 **Example:**

- **A couple who argues but always finds a way to reconnect is using stubbornness in a healthy way.**
- **A person who stays in a toxic relationship, hoping things will change, is using stubbornness in a self-destructive way.**

◈ **Lesson: Stubbornness should build love, not destroy it.**

2. Why Stubborn People Struggle in Relationships

✔ Stubborn people are often **independent, strong-willed, and opinionated.**

✔ This can make relationships challenging if they:

- Refuse to compromise.
- Prioritize being right over being happy.
- Struggle to apologize or admit fault.

💡 **Example:**

- **Steve Jobs was famously stubborn in business and personal life—his inability to admit mistakes hurt many of his closest relationships.**

◈ **Lesson: Love requires strength, but also flexibility.**

Phase 2: When to Hold On—Fighting for Love That's Worth It

1. The Power of Commitment—Why Love Requires Stubborn Effort

✔ **Great relationships don't just happen—they require work.**

✔ Every long-term couple goes through **periods of difficulty, doubt, and frustration.**

💡 **Example:**

- **Barack and Michelle Obama openly share how their marriage was tested over the years, but they stayed committed and grew stronger together.**

◈ **Action Step:**

✔ When times get tough, ask: *"Is this a challenge we can work through, or is it a sign to walk away?"*

2. The "Two Non-Negotiables" Rule

✔ Stubborn love works when both partners agree on two core values they will never compromise on.

✔ These could be:

- **Loyalty and honesty.**
- **Support during hard times.**
- **Growth and learning together.**

💡 **Example:**

- **Will Smith and Jada Pinkett Smith built their marriage on the idea of "ride or die"—staying together through struggles but always evolving.**

◈ **Action Step:**

✔ Identify **two non-negotiable values** that define your relationship.

3. How to Be Stubborn Without Being Controlling

✔ There's a difference between **fighting for love** and **trying to control someone.**

✔ Healthy stubbornness means:

- Letting your partner grow as an individual.
- Encouraging open communication, not forcing your opinions.

💡 **Example:**

- **Beyoncé and Jay-Z worked through struggles in their marriage by focusing on growth rather than control.**

◈ **Action Step:**

✔ Ask yourself: *"Am I fighting for us, or am I trying to change them?"*

Phase 3: When to Let Go—Recognizing When Love No Longer Serves You

1. The "No More Excuses" Rule

✔ Stubbornness becomes dangerous when it **keeps you stuck in an unhealthy relationship.**

✔ Ask yourself:

- *"Am I holding on because I believe in us, or because I'm afraid to be alone?"*
- *"Am I waiting for something to change that never will?"*

💡 **Example:**

- **Many people stay in toxic relationships because they hope things will improve, but deep down, they know they won't.**

◈ **Lesson: Letting go is sometimes the bravest form of stubbornness.**

2. How to Know When It's Time to Walk Away

✘ **If a relationship consistently makes you feel drained, unworthy, or anxious, it's time to leave.**

✘ **If your partner refuses to grow, change, or take responsibility, your stubborn love won't fix them.**

💡 **Example:**

- **Maya Angelou famously said, "When someone shows you who they are, believe them the first time."**

◈ **Action Step:**

✔ If you've been **waiting for years** for someone to change, ask yourself: *"How much longer am I willing to wait?"*

Phase 4: How to Balance Stubbornness and Love

1. The "Pick Your Battles" Strategy

✔ Not every disagreement needs to be won.

✔ Ask: *"Is this argument worth it, or can I let it go?"*

💡 **Example:**

- **Happily married couples focus on important issues—not petty arguments.**

◈ **Action Step:**

✔ Before fighting, pause and ask yourself: *"Will this matter in five years?"*

2. The Power of Apologizing Without Weakness

✔ Apologizing doesn't mean you're weak—it means you value the relationship.

✔ Stubborn people often struggle to say "I'm sorry."

💡 **Example:**

- **Dwayne "The Rock" Johnson admits he used to let his ego hurt relationships but learned that apologizing actually makes him stronger.**

◈ **Action Step:**

✔ Practice saying:

- *"I see your point."*
- *"I was wrong."*
- *"I care about us more than my pride."*

3. The "Give and Take" Approach

✔ If both partners are equally stubborn, compromise is essential.

✔ **Make sure stubbornness doesn't turn into a constant power struggle.**

💡 **Example:**

- **Chrissy Teigen and John Legend talk about balancing strong personalities in their marriage through compromise.**

◈ **Action Step:**

✔ Ask: *"Where can I bend without losing myself?"*

Phase 5: Exercises to Strengthen or Release a Relationship

1. The "Why Are We Together?" Test

✔ Write down **5 reasons you're in this relationship.**

✔ If they are all based on fear, loneliness, or obligation, it may be time to let go.

2. The "Growth Check-In" Exercise

✔ Ask your partner:

- *"How do you feel about where we are?"*
- *"How can we improve?"*

💡 **Lesson: A great relationship requires two people actively choosing each other, not just coasting.**

3. The "Walking Away" Visualization

✔ Imagine what life would be like if you left.

✔ If you feel **relief instead of sadness**, it may be time to move on.

Conclusion: Stubborn Love Should Build, Not Destroy

✔ **Be stubborn about love that's worth it—but strong enough to leave love that isn't.**

✔ **The right kind of stubbornness keeps a relationship together, while the wrong kind keeps you stuck.**

✔ **Love is a choice—make sure you're choosing wisely.**

💡 *"Sometimes the bravest thing you can do is fight for love. Other times, it's walking away."*

🚀 **Next Chapter:** How to Be Stubborn Without Being Toxic—Balancing Strength and Understanding.

CHAPTER 18

How to Be Stubborn Without Being Toxic—Balancing Strength and Understanding

> **"Strong people don't put others down—they lift them up."**
>
> — Michael P. Watson

Introduction: Stubbornness vs. Toxicity

Stubbornness is powerful when used correctly, but **it can easily become toxic if left unchecked.**

✔ **Healthy stubbornness** helps you stand your ground and stay committed.

✕ **Toxic stubbornness** makes you rigid, unapproachable, and difficult to be around.

💡 **This chapter will teach you how to balance stubbornness with wisdom, ensuring that your persistence strengthens your relationships instead of harming them.**

Phase 1: Understanding the Difference Between Strength and Toxicity

1. When Stubbornness Becomes Toxic

✔ **Healthy Stubbornness Means:**

- Standing by your values but staying open to new perspectives.
- Being determined without being disrespectful.
- Knowing when to compromise for the greater good.

✕ **Toxic Stubbornness Looks Like:**

- Refusing to listen or consider other viewpoints.
- Turning every disagreement into a battle.
- Letting pride or ego control your actions.

💡 **Example:**

- **Michael Jordan was famously stubborn in his pursuit of greatness—but he also learned how to be a leader instead of just a competitor.**

◈ **Lesson: Stubbornness should help you grow, not alienate others.**

2. Why Some People Confuse Stubbornness with Strength

✔ Many people mistake **being stubborn for being "strong."**

✔ But true strength means knowing:

- When to stand firm.
- When to listen.
- When to walk away.

💡 **Example:**

- **Steve Jobs was known for his stubborn perfectionism, which led to great products—but also made him difficult to work with.**

◈ **Lesson: Being too rigid can hurt your success as much as giving up too easily.**

Phase 2: How to Stay Stubborn Without Pushing People Away

1. Master the Art of Selective Stubbornness

✔ Not every battle needs to be fought.

✔ Choose **which things truly matter** and let the rest go.

💡 **Example:**

- **Successful leaders focus on big-picture goals, not petty arguments.**

◈ **Action Step:**

✔ Before being stubborn about something, ask:

- *"Is this really worth it?"*
- *"Will this matter a year from now?"*

2. Learn to Listen Without Feeling Threatened

✔ Many stubborn people **get defensive** when challenged.

✔ But listening doesn't mean **agreeing—it means understanding.**

💡 **Example:**

- **Barack Obama built his leadership on listening before making decisions—showing strength without aggression.**

◈ **Action Step:**

✔ Practice saying:

- *"I see your point, let me think about it."*

3. The "Pause Before You React" Rule

✔ Stubborn people often react too quickly in debates.

✔ **Pausing** before responding makes you appear more confident and rational.

💡 **Example:**

- **Warren Buffett is famous for his ability to stay calm and thoughtful during negotiations.**

◈ **Action Step:**

✔ When someone challenges you, **pause for 5 seconds before responding.**

Phase 3: How to Stand Your Ground Without Being Overbearing

1. Set Boundaries Without Being Aggressive

✔ Being firm **doesn't mean being rude.**

✔ The best boundary-setters are **calm, clear, and consistent.**

💡 **Example:**

- **Oprah Winfrey is known for setting strong boundaries without disrespecting others.**

◈ **Action Step:**

✔ Instead of saying, *"No, I won't do that!"*

- Say, *"That doesn't work for me, but here's what I can do."*

2. Replace Pride with Purpose

✔ Stubbornness becomes toxic when it's driven by **ego instead of values.**

✔ Before refusing something, ask:

- *"Am I standing my ground because this is important, or just because I want to be right?"*

💡 **Example:**

- **Mark Cuban built his success on persistence but admits he had to learn when to let go of bad business ideas.**

◈ **Lesson: Stand firm for what matters, not just to prove a point.**

3. How to Argue Without Destroying Relationships

✔ **Disagreements are normal, but how you handle them matters.**

✔ Instead of trying to "win" an argument, aim to **understand and be understood.**

💡 **Example:**

- **Healthy couples argue with the goal of resolution, not to "defeat" each other.**

◈ **Action Step:**

✔ Instead of saying, *"You're wrong!"*

- Say, *"I see it differently. Let's find a solution together."*

Phase 4: How to Recognize When You're Being Too Stubborn

1. The "3 Strikes" Rule

✔ If **three different people** tell you the same thing about yourself, it's time to reflect.

💡 **Example:**

- **If multiple people say you're too closed-minded, it's worth considering.**

◈ **Action Step:**

✔ Write down the last three times someone called you stubborn. Were they right?

2. The "What's the Cost?" Question

✔ Ask yourself:

- *"Is my stubbornness helping me or holding me back?"*
- *"Is this fight worth losing a relationship over?"*

💡 **Lesson: If your stubbornness is hurting more than helping, adjust.**

3. Learning to Say "I Was Wrong" Without Losing Power

✔ Many stubborn people fear **admitting mistakes.**

✔ But **owning up to errors** actually makes you stronger.

💡 **Example:**

- **Successful leaders like Richard Branson openly admit when they're wrong, making them more respected.**

◈ **Action Step:**

✔ Practice saying:

- *"I was wrong about that, and I appreciate your perspective."*

Phase 5: Exercises to Balance Stubbornness with Understanding

1. The "Stubborn Priorities" List

✔ Write down **three things you should always be stubborn about.**

✔ Then write down **three things you should be more flexible about.**

💡 **Lesson: Not everything requires 100% stubbornness.**

2. The "Silent Listener" Challenge

✔ Pick one conversation where you just **listen without responding immediately.**

✔ Notice how much better you understand the other person.

💡 **Lesson: Pausing before reacting builds trust and respect.**

3. The "Let It Go" Experiment

✔ Choose **one thing this week** that you would normally argue about and **let it go instead.**

✔ Notice if the outcome is actually better.

💡 **Lesson: Sometimes, backing down is the smarter move.**

Conclusion: Stubbornness Should Be a Strength, Not a Weakness

✔ **Being stubborn is powerful—but only when used correctly.**

✔ **The best people know when to fight and when to listen.**

✔ **Control your stubbornness, or it will control you.**

💡 *"Strong people don't prove their strength by refusing to change—they prove it by knowing when to."*

🚀 **Next Chapter:** Standing Your Ground—How to Say No and Mean It.

CHAPTER 19

Standing Your Ground—How to Say No and Mean It

> **"The difference between successful people and really successful people is that really successful people say no to almost everything."**
>
> — Warren Buffett

Introduction: Why Most People Struggle to Say No

Saying "no" is one of the most powerful skills you can develop.

✔ **It protects your time, energy, and priorities.**

✔ **It prevents you from being manipulated or overworked.**

✔ **It allows you to stay focused on what truly matters.**

But most people struggle to say no because:

✘ They don't want to disappoint others.

✘ They fear conflict or rejection.

✘ They feel guilty for prioritizing themselves.

💡 **This chapter will teach you how to say no with confidence—without guilt, fear, or unnecessary conflict.**

Phase 1: Why Saying No is a Superpower

1. The Hidden Cost of Always Saying Yes

✔ Every time you say **yes** to something you don't want to do, you are saying **no** to something more important.

✔ Saying yes out of guilt leads to **burnout, frustration, and resentment.**

💡 **Example:**

- **Elon Musk says no to most meetings, calls, and distractions—allowing him to focus on innovation.**

◈ **Lesson: The most successful people are selective about what they say yes to.**

2. Why People Manipulate You Into Saying Yes

✔ Some people take advantage of **your kindness or fear of conflict.**

✔ Common manipulation tactics:

- **Guilt-tripping** ("If you cared about me, you'd do it.")
- **Fake urgency** ("I need this right now!")
- **Social pressure** ("Everyone else is doing it.")

💡 **Example:**

- **Steve Jobs was a master at saying no to bad ideas, even when pressured by his team.**

◈ **Lesson: If saying yes makes you feel trapped, it's a sign you need to say no.**

Phase 2: The Art of Saying No Without Feeling Guilty

1. The "Firm but Kind" Technique

✔ You don't have to be rude—you just need to be clear.

✔ **Example responses:**

- *"I appreciate the offer, but I can't commit to that right now."*
- *"I have other priorities, so I have to decline."*

💡 **Example:**

- **Oprah Winfrey built her success by learning to say no to distractions.**

◈ **Action Step:**

✔ The next time you feel pressured, use one of the responses above.

2. The "Broken Record" Strategy

✔ Some people won't take no for an answer.

✔ Repeat your response **without explaining or justifying yourself.**

💡 **Example:**

- **If someone keeps pushing you, say: "I understand, but my answer is still no."**

◈ **Action Step:**

✔ Practice saying no **without over-explaining.**

3. Use "No" as a Redirection

✔ If you want to soften your no, **offer an alternative.**

💡 **Example:**

- *"I can't help with that, but I can recommend someone who might."*

◈ **Action Step:**

✔ Find a way to say no **without burning bridges.**

Phase 3: How to Say No in Different Situations

1. Saying No to Friends & Family

✔ **Common challenge:** Feeling guilty for letting loved ones down.

✔ **Solution:** Be honest, but firm.

💡 **Example:**

- Instead of:

✕ *"I guess I'll do it, even though I don't want to."*

☑ Say: *"I love you, but I can't commit to that right now."*

◈ **Lesson: You can love people and still set boundaries.**

2. Saying No at Work

✔ **Common challenge:** Fear of looking uncooperative.

✔ **Solution:** Offer a reason without apologizing.

💡 **Example:**

- Instead of:

✕ *"I'm too busy, sorry."*

☑ Say: *"I can't take this on, but I can revisit it next month."*

◈ **Lesson: Protect your time without damaging professional relationships.**

3. Saying No to Manipulative People

✔ **Common challenge:** People who won't take no for an answer.

✔ **Solution:** Use the "broken record" technique.

💡 **Example:**

- If they keep pushing, say:

☑ *"I understand, but my decision is final."*

◈ **Lesson: Refusing to argue takes away their power.**

Phase 4: How to Strengthen Your "No" Muscle

1. The "Daily No" Challenge

✔ **Practice saying no** to small things every day.

✔ The more you do it, the easier it gets.

💡 **Example:**

- **Start by declining unnecessary emails, small favors, or unimportant meetings.**

◈ **Lesson: Saying no gets easier with repetition.**

2. The "Will This Help My Goals?" Test

✔ Before saying yes, ask:

- *"Does this align with my long-term goals?"*

✔ If not, say no.

💡 **Example:**

- **Billionaire investor Warren Buffett says no to almost everything that doesn't help his business.**

💎 **Lesson: Protect your priorities like your life depends on it.**

3. The "Write Your Boundaries" Exercise

✔ List **three things you will start saying no to.**

✔ Keep this list visible as a reminder.

💡 **Lesson: When you know your boundaries, saying no becomes automatic.**

Conclusion: No is a Complete Sentence

✔ **Saying no doesn't make you selfish—it makes you strong.**

✔ **Every time you say no to something that drains you, you're saying yes to something that fulfills you.**

✔ **If you don't protect your time, others will waste it.**

💡 *"The ability to say no is the key to success, freedom, and peace of mind."*

🚀 **Next Chapter:** How to Convince Others to See Your Vision Without Forcing It.

CHAPTER 20

How to Convince Others to See Your Vision Without Forcing It

"People don't buy what you do, they buy why you do it."

— Simon Sinek

Introduction: Why Forcing People to Agree Never Works

Many people **struggle to get others to believe in their vision** because they:

❌ Try to **force** their ideas onto others.

❌ Get frustrated when people don't immediately agree.

❌ Give up when they face resistance.

✔ **But true leaders don't force—they inspire.**

✔ **They know how to make people believe in their vision without manipulation or pressure.**

💡 **This chapter will teach you how to make others believe in your vision—without pushing, arguing, or begging for approval.**

Phase 1: Why People Resist Your Vision (And How to Overcome It)

1. Understanding Why People Say No to New Ideas

✔ Most people resist change—not because your idea is bad, but because:

- They fear the unknown.
- They don't want to look wrong.
- They are comfortable with the status quo.

💡 **Example:**

- **When the Wright brothers first talked about flying, people thought they were crazy.**

◈ **Lesson: People don't resist ideas—they resist change.**

2. The Psychology of Persuasion: Why Logic Alone Doesn't Work

✔ Facts don't convince people—**emotions do.**

✔ If you want people to believe in your vision, **connect to their emotions, not just their minds.**

💡 **Example:**

- **Steve Jobs didn't sell computers—he sold a vision of creativity and innovation.**

◈ **Lesson: People don't buy ideas—they buy feelings.**

3. Why Trying to "Prove" Yourself Backfires

✔ The more you **argue and push**, the more people resist.

✔ Instead of **forcing your vision, invite them to see the possibilities.**

💡 **Example:**

- **Jeff Bezos didn't beg people to believe in Amazon—he just showed results over time.**

◈ **Lesson: If you keep proving your vision, people will eventually believe in it.**

Phase 2: How to Get People to Believe in Your Vision

1. The "Show, Don't Tell" Rule

✔ Instead of telling people why your vision is great, **let your actions prove it.**

✔ People trust results more than promises.

💡 **Example:**

- **Elon Musk didn't just talk about reusable rockets—he built one and made it land.**

◈ **Action Step:**

✔ Focus on **doing the work first—people will follow once they see results.**

2. Speak in Stories, Not Just Facts

✔ People remember **stories** more than they remember statistics.

✔ If you want people to believe in your vision, **tell them a story that connects to their emotions.**

💡 **Example:**

- **Martin Luther King Jr. didn't give a "plan"—he gave a "dream."**

◈ **Action Step:**

✔ When sharing your vision, **use personal stories to make it relatable.**

3. Find the Right People First

✔ Some people will never believe in your vision—and that's okay.

✔ Instead of convincing everyone, **find those who are already open to new ideas.**

💡 **Example:**

- **Early Tesla investors believed in Musk's vision, while others laughed—today, Tesla is worth billions.**

◈ **Action Step:**

✔ Stop wasting energy on people who don't believe—**focus on those who do.**

Phase 3: How to Get People Excited About Your Vision

1. The "Why Should They Care?" Test

✔ People only care about your vision if it benefits them.

✔ **Before sharing your idea, ask:**

- *"Why should this person care?"*
- *"How does my vision help them?"*

💡 **Example:**

- **Steve Jobs didn't sell the iPhone as a product—he sold it as a way to simplify life.**

◈ **Action Step:**

✔ Frame your vision around **how it benefits the other person.**

2. Use the Power of Curiosity

✔ People are more likely to listen when they are **curious.**

✔ Instead of telling people everything upfront, **give them a reason to ask questions.**

💡 **Example:**

- **Instead of saying, "This will change the world," say, "What if there was a way to make life 10X easier?"**

◈ **Action Step:**

✔ Ask **intriguing questions** that make people want to know more.

3. Let People Feel Like It's Their Idea

✔ People resist being told what to do—but they love **being part of something new.**

✔ Instead of **forcing your idea, let people contribute to it.**

💡 **Example:**

- **Google's best innovations come from employees, not just leadership.**

◈ **Action Step:**

✔ Make people feel **involved** in your vision, not just an audience to it.

Phase 4: How to Handle Skeptics and Doubters

1. The "Watch Me" Strategy

✔ Instead of arguing with doubters, **prove them wrong through results.**

✔ Let your success be your response.

💡 **Example:**

- **Oprah was told she wasn't fit for TV—she didn't argue, she just became a billionaire.**

◈ **Action Step:**

✔ When someone doubts you, just say: *"Watch me."*

2. Turn Rejection Into Motivation

✔ If people don't believe in you now, **use it as fuel to work even harder.**

💡 **Example:**

- **Michael Jordan was cut from his high school team—he used it as motivation to become the greatest player of all time.**

◈ **Lesson: Doubt should push you forward, not hold you back.**

3. Let Time Do the Talking

✔ Some people will only believe in your vision **after they see proof.**

✔ Instead of wasting time convincing them, **focus on building.**

💡 **Example:**

- **Every major innovation (cars, planes, the internet) was laughed at before it became reality.**

◈ **Lesson: What people doubt today, they will believe tomorrow—if you keep going.**

Phase 5: Exercises to Strengthen Your Influence

1. The "One-Sentence Vision" Challenge

✔ **Write your vision in one clear sentence.**

✔ If you can't explain it simply, **it's too complicated.**

💡 **Lesson: Simplicity makes people believe faster.**

2. The "Ask More, Talk Less" Rule

✔ Instead of **telling** people what to think, **ask them questions.**

✔ When people feel heard, they are more open to new ideas.

💡 **Example:**

- **Instead of saying, "You should believe in this," ask, "What do you think about this idea?"**

◈ **Lesson: People support what they help create.**

3. The "Test Your Vision" Experiment

✔ Share your vision with **three different types of people:**

- A close friend
- A skeptic
- A complete stranger

✔ See how they react and **refine your approach.**

💡 **Lesson: The way you communicate your vision matters as much as the vision itself.**

Conclusion: Inspire, Don't Force

✔ **People believe in leaders who believe in themselves.**

✔ **You don't need to force people to see your vision—just keep proving it.**

✔ **The world always doubts new ideas until they become reality.**

💡 *"First they ignore you, then they laugh at you, then they fight you, then you win."* – Mahatma Gandhi

🚀 **Next Chapter:** The Stubborn Entrepreneur—How the Most Successful People Build Businesses That Last.

CHAPTER 21

The Stubborn Entrepreneur—How the Most Successful People Build Businesses That Last

"The most successful entrepreneurs are not the most talented—they are the most relentless."

— Unknown

Introduction: Why Stubbornness is the Secret to Entrepreneurial Success

Starting and growing a business is **not about luck, intelligence, or even funding.**

It's about **stubbornly refusing to give up—even when everything seems impossible.**

✔ **Most businesses fail because the founder quits too soon.**

✔ **The ones that succeed do so because their leaders push through every obstacle.**

💡 **This chapter will teach you how to harness your stubbornness to build a business that survives, thrives, and lasts.**

Phase 1: The Mindset of a Stubborn Entrepreneur

1. Why Most Entrepreneurs Give Up Too Soon

✔ **The #1 reason businesses fail is not lack of funding, but lack of persistence.**

✔ Many entrepreneurs quit because they:

- Expect success to happen too quickly.
- Get discouraged after early failures.
- Let doubt and criticism get to them.

💡 **Example:**

- **Jeff Bezos lost millions in Amazon's early years—but he stubbornly believed in e-commerce, and today Amazon dominates the world.**

◈ **Lesson: Success takes time—stubbornness keeps you in the game long enough to win.**

2. The Difference Between Good and Bad Stubbornness in Business

✔ **Good stubbornness:** Sticking to your vision despite setbacks.

✔ **Bad stubbornness:** Refusing to adapt when something clearly isn't working.

💡 **Example:**

- **Netflix pivoted from DVDs to streaming when the market changed. Blockbuster refused—and died.**

◈ **Lesson: Be stubborn about your goals, but flexible about how you achieve them.**

3. How to Develop a Never-Quit Mentality

✔ Every great entrepreneur has faced failure:

- **Elon Musk nearly went bankrupt before Tesla succeeded.**
- **Howard Schultz was rejected by over 200 investors before Starbucks took off.**

◈ **Action Step:**

✔ Instead of asking, *"What if I fail?"* ask, *"What if I never quit?"*

Phase 2: How to Stay Stubborn Through the Toughest Challenges

1. How to Handle Rejection Without Losing Confidence

✔ Expect **rejection**—it's a normal part of business.

✔ **Instead of taking it personally, treat it as a numbers game.**

💡 **Example:**

- **Colonel Sanders pitched KFC to over 1,000 restaurants before one said yes.**

◈ **Action Step:**

✔ **Set a rejection goal.** Aim for **50 rejections** before assuming your idea won't work.

2. How to Push Through Financial Struggles

✔ Most businesses struggle with **cash flow in the early years.**

✔ The key is **stubborn resourcefulness—finding ways to keep going even with little money.**

💡 **Example:**

- **Sara Blakely (Spanx founder) started with no funding—she stubbornly bootstrapped her way to a billion-dollar brand.**

◈ **Action Step:**

✔ **Instead of saying, "I don't have enough money," ask, "How can I make this work with what I have?"**

3. How to Keep Going When No One Believes in Your Vision

✔ Most groundbreaking ideas **start with people laughing at them.**

✔ If people doubt you, **you're probably on the right track.**

💡 **Example:**

- **Henry Ford's idea of cars for everyone was mocked—until he changed the world.**

◈ **Action Step:**

✔ The next time someone doubts your business, say: *"Great—another reason to prove them wrong."*

Phase 3: The Daily Stubborn Habits of Successful Entrepreneurs

1. The "One More Day" Rule

✔ When you feel like quitting, **just commit to one more day.**

✔ 99% of success is simply **outlasting the competition.**

💡 **Example:**

- **Thomas Edison kept experimenting daily—until the light bulb finally worked.**

◈ **Action Step:**

✔ Every time you want to quit, tell yourself: *"I'll just try one more day."*

2. The "No Plan B" Commitment

✔ Many entrepreneurs fail because they **have a backup plan.**

✔ If you truly want to succeed, **burn the boats—make success your only option.**

💡 **Example:**

- **Arnold Schwarzenegger never had a "backup plan"—he made his dreams non-negotiable.**

◈ **Action Step:**

✔ Remove "maybe" from your goals—make them musts.

3. The "Micro-Progress" Strategy

✔ Instead of waiting for **huge success,** focus on **small wins every day.**

✔ **Small stubborn efforts compound into massive results.**

💡 **Example:**

- **Amazon started with just books—Bezos stubbornly expanded one step at a time.**

◈ **Action Step:**

✔ Every day, ask: *"What's one small step I can take today?"*

Phase 4: How to Handle Failure Like a Stubborn Entrepreneur

1. How to Stop Taking Failure Personally

✔ **Failure is feedback, not a final verdict.**

✔ Every great entrepreneur has failed—but they learned from it.

💡 **Example:**

- **Oprah was fired from her first TV job—now she runs a media empire.**

◈ **Action Step:**

✔ Instead of saying, *"I failed,"* say, *"I just learned what doesn't work."*

2. The "Bounce-Back Faster" Formula

✔ The best entrepreneurs **don't dwell on failure—they adapt fast.**

✔ **Speed of recovery = speed of success.**

💡 **Example:**

- **Bill Gates' first company failed—but he pivoted and built Microsoft.**

◈ **Action Step:**

✔ When you fail, ask: *"What can I adjust and try again immediately?"*

3. Why Quitting Too Soon is the Biggest Mistake

✔ **Most people quit just before they succeed.**

✔ If you **hold out longer than others, you win by default.**

💡 **Example:**

- **Walt Disney was rejected 302 times before getting funding for Disneyland.**

◈ **Lesson: If you can outlast failure, success is inevitable.**

Phase 5: Exercises to Strengthen Entrepreneurial Stubbornness

1. The "50 Rejections" Challenge

✔ Get **50 rejections** before even considering giving up.

✔ Treat rejection as a milestone, not a failure.

💡 **Lesson: The more you embrace rejection, the closer you are to success.**

2. The "Survivor's List" Exercise

✔ Write down **5 legendary entrepreneurs** who refused to quit.

✔ Read their stories every time you feel like giving up.

💡 **Lesson: Success leaves clues—follow those who persisted.**

3. The "Why I Won't Quit" Letter

✔ Write a letter to yourself explaining **why you will never give up.**

✔ Read it whenever doubt creeps in.

💡 **Lesson: Your stubborn commitment will keep you going.**

Conclusion: Build a Business That Lasts by Refusing to Give Up

✔ **The world belongs to the entrepreneurs who refuse to quit.**

✔ **Most businesses fail—not because the idea was bad, but because the founder gave up too soon.**

✔ **If you can survive the early struggles, success will come.**

💡 *"The secret to success is to stay in the game long enough to win."*

🚀 **Next Chapter:** How to Handle Office Politics Without Losing Your Integrity.

CHAPTER 22

How to Handle Office Politics Without Losing Your Integrity

"The key to office politics is knowing when to play the game and when to rise above it."

— Unknown

Introduction: Why Office Politics Exist (And How to Navigate Them Without Compromising Yourself)

In every workplace, **office politics exist**—even in the best companies.

✔ Some people play dirty to get ahead.

✔ Others manipulate, gossip, and take credit for work they didn't do.

✔ Many good employees get left behind because they refuse to engage in politics.

But here's the truth:

✔ You **can't ignore** office politics—but you **can** play them strategically while keeping your integrity.

💡 **This chapter will teach you how to navigate workplace politics like a pro—without becoming someone you're not.**

Phase 1: Understanding the Game Without Becoming a Pawn

1. Why Office Politics Exist (And Why Ignoring Them Hurts You)

✔ Politics happen in every workplace because:

- **People want influence, power, and recognition.**
- **Not everyone plays fair.**
- **Some people will do anything to climb the corporate ladder.**

💡 **Example:**

- **Many talented employees get overlooked because they think "hard work speaks for itself."**

◈ **Lesson: If you ignore office politics, you may lose opportunities to those who don't.**

2. The Difference Between Playing Smart and Playing Dirty

✔ **Smart office politics = Building influence with integrity.**

✔ **Dirty office politics = Manipulation, backstabbing, and dishonesty.**

💡 **Example:**

- **Sheryl Sandberg (former COO of Facebook) built strong relationships in leadership—not by gossiping, but by making herself valuable.**

◈ **Lesson: You don't have to play dirty to win—you just have to play smart.**

3. Why Being "Too Nice" Can Hold You Back

✔ Many people avoid politics because they **don't want to be seen as "political."**

✔ But **being too nice or too silent** can get you ignored.

💡 **Example:**

- **If you never speak up in meetings, someone else will take credit for your ideas.**

◈ **Lesson: You can be kind AND assertive at the same time.**

Phase 2: How to Navigate Office Politics Without Losing Yourself

1. Build Influence Without Gossiping

✔ Avoid office gossip—it will always backfire.

✔ Instead, **build genuine relationships based on trust.**

💡 **Example:**

- **Oprah Winfrey built her media empire by focusing on authenticity, not backstabbing.**

◈ **Action Step:**

✔ If someone starts gossiping, change the subject or walk away.

2. Make Yourself Invaluable (So Politics Don't Control Your Career)

✔ The best way to **win in office politics** is to be so valuable that people respect you—whether they like you or not.

✔ **Be the person who solves problems, not creates them.**

💡 **Example:**

- **Jeff Bezos was relentless about results—his value made him impossible to ignore.**

◈ **Action Step:**

✔ Focus on delivering **high-impact work** that no one else can do.

3. The "Speak Last" Rule (How to Gain Respect Without Fighting for It)

✔ **People who speak last in meetings are often seen as the most powerful.**

✔ Listen first, then add **a well-thought-out, impactful comment.**

💡 **Example:**

- **Barack Obama is known for listening carefully before speaking—giving his words more weight.**

◈ **Action Step:**

✔ In your next meeting, **wait before speaking—then make your point concisely.**

Phase 3: How to Protect Yourself from Toxic Politics

1. Spot the Political Players Early

✔ Some people in the office **thrive on politics and manipulation.**

✔ **Recognizing them early can help you avoid their traps.**

💡 **Example:**

- **Look out for co-workers who always take credit for others' work.**

◈ **Action Step:**

✔ If someone tries to steal your work, keep a **written record of your contributions.**

2. The Art of Saying No Without Making Enemies

✔ **You don't have to do everything just to be liked.**

✔ Say no in a way that **keeps relationships intact.**

💡 **Example:**

- Instead of saying:
- ✕ *"I don't have time for that."*

☑ Say: *"I'd love to help, but I have to focus on higher-priority tasks."*

◈ **Action Step:**

✔ The next time someone asks you for extra work, **practice saying no politely but firmly.**

3. How to Handle a Toxic Boss or Colleague

✔ If you have **a toxic boss or co-worker,** document everything.

✔ If things escalate, **go to HR with evidence—not just complaints.**

💡 **Example:**

- **Many employees stay stuck in bad situations because they don't document proof.**

◈ **Action Step:**

✔ Keep **emails, meeting notes, and examples of toxic behavior.**

Phase 4: How to Rise in the Workplace Without Playing Dirty

1. Build Allies, Not Enemies

✔ You don't have to be **friends with everyone—but you should have workplace allies.**

✔ A strong **network protects you from office politics.**

💡 **Example:**

- **Successful leaders surround themselves with people who support their growth.**

◈ **Action Step:**

✔ Identify **three key people** in your workplace who can be allies.

2. Get Credit for Your Work (Without Bragging)

✔ Many people **work hard but never get noticed** because they don't showcase their value.

✔ **Instead of bragging, document your wins and share them strategically.**

💡 **Example:**

- **Women in the White House used a strategy called "amplification" to ensure their ideas were heard.**

◈ **Action Step:**

✔ Keep a **success journal** and bring it up in meetings or performance reviews.

3. Use Emotional Intelligence to Stay Ahead

✔ **People skills matter as much as hard work.**

✔ Learn to **read people's motivations and adapt accordingly.**

💡 **Example:**

- **Bill Gates wasn't the most charismatic, but he understood human nature well enough to build Microsoft.**

◈ **Action Step:**

✔ Improve **your emotional intelligence** by observing workplace dynamics.

Phase 5: Exercises to Master Office Politics Without Losing Integrity

1. The "Observe Before You Act" Challenge

✔ For one week, **just observe workplace politics without reacting.**

✔ Notice **who holds power, who influences decisions, and how people navigate conversations.**

💡 **Lesson: Understanding the game makes it easier to win.**

2. The "Relationship Building" Experiment

✔ Pick **one influential person** in your company and **build a professional relationship with them.**

✔ Offer **value** instead of just asking for favors.

💡 **Lesson: Who you know can be just as important as what you do.**

3. The "Protect Your Work" Strategy

✔ Keep **a private document** of your contributions, wins, and ideas.

✔ Use this in performance reviews to ensure you get credit.

💡 **Lesson: If you don't track your wins, someone else might take them.**

Conclusion: Master Office Politics Without Losing Yourself

✔ **You don't have to be fake to succeed—you just have to be smart.**

✔ **Recognize the game, but don't become the game.**

✔ **Your best defense against politics is being so valuable that no one can ignore you.**

💡 *"Integrity is doing the right thing, even when no one is watching."*

🚀 **Next Chapter:** Becoming Indispensable—Why Stubborn Employees Get Promoted.

CHAPTER 23

Becoming Indispensable—Why Stubborn Employees Get Promoted

> **"If you want to be irreplaceable, you have to bring something no one else does."**
>
> — Steve Jobs

Introduction: Why Some Employees Get Promoted While Others Stay Stuck

Most people believe that promotions are based on **hard work and talent.**

❌ **That's a myth.**

✔ The employees who get promoted are **not always the smartest or hardest working**—they are the ones who are **stubbornly strategic** about their growth.

✔ **They make themselves indispensable.**

💡 **This chapter will teach you how to become the kind of employee that companies can't afford to ignore—or lose.**

Phase 1: Why Hard Work Alone Won't Get You Promoted

1. The Harsh Truth About Career Growth

✔ Most employees think that **doing good work is enough.**

✔ In reality, **if no one notices your work, it doesn't exist.**

💡 **Example:**

- **Many people work late nights but never get promoted—because they don't position themselves correctly.**

◈ **Lesson: Hard work without visibility = career stagnation.**

2. Why Some Employees Rise Faster Than Others

✔ They know how to **market their contributions.**

✔ They build **strong relationships with decision-makers.**

✔ They take on **high-value work** (not just busy work).

💡 **Example:**

- **Jeff Bezos wasn't the most brilliant person in his company—but he was the most persistent and strategic.**

◈ **Lesson: It's not about working harder—it's about working smarter.**

3. The Three Types of Employees (Which One Are You?)

✔ **The Invisible Worker** – Works hard but goes unnoticed.

✔ **The Team Player** – Well-liked but replaceable.

✔ **The Indispensable Employee** – A problem-solver who drives results.

💡 **Example:**

- **Sheryl Sandberg (former COO of Facebook) made herself indispensable by solving big problems—not just working long hours.**

◈ **Action Step:**

✔ **Move from being "hardworking" to being "high-impact."**

Phase 2: How to Make Yourself Indispensable

1. Become the Go-To Problem Solver

✔ Companies promote **employees who solve big problems.**

✔ Stop focusing on tasks—**start solving issues that make an impact.**

💡 **Example:**

- **Indra Nooyi (former CEO of Pepsi) didn't just do her job—she identified key business gaps and fixed them.**

◈ **Action Step:**

✔ **Identify one major problem in your company—and work on a solution.**

2. Own a Unique Skill That No One Else Has

✔ The more **specialized your skill set,** the harder it is to replace you.

✔ **Learn something valuable that others don't know.**

💡 **Example:**

- **Elon Musk taught himself rocket science—making himself indispensable at SpaceX.**

◈ **Action Step:**

✔ Ask: *"What skill can I develop that will make me stand out?"*

3. Control Your Own Career Narrative

✔ If you don't **define your value, someone else will.**

✔ Talk about your achievements **without bragging.**

💡 **Example:**

- Instead of saying, *"I worked hard on this project,"*

☑ Say: *"This project increased revenue by 20%."*

◈ **Action Step:**

✔ **Keep a record of your wins and share them at the right time.**

Phase 3: The Stubborn Work Ethic That Gets You Promoted

1. The "Make Your Boss's Job Easier" Trick

✔ The fastest way to get promoted? **Make your boss's life easier.**

✔ Solve problems before they even notice them.

💡 **Example:**

- **Satya Nadella (CEO of Microsoft) was promoted because he focused on results, not office politics.**

◈ **Action Step:**

✔ Ask: *"What's one thing I can do to make my boss's job easier?"*

2. Take Initiative Before Being Asked

✔ Waiting to be told what to do = **staying replaceable.**

✔ Taking initiative **before being asked = leadership potential.**

💡 **Example:**

- **Howard Schultz (Starbucks) didn't wait to be CEO—he started leading before he had the title.**

◈ **Action Step:**

✔ Start working at the **next level** before you get promoted.

3. Speak Up in Meetings (Even If You're Introverted)

✔ If you're silent, **people assume you have nothing to contribute.**

✔ Even if you say just **one smart thing per meeting,** it raises your visibility.

💡 **Example:**

- **Billionaire investor Ray Dalio encourages employees to challenge ideas, not just agree.**

◈ **Action Step:**

✔ Aim to contribute **at least one insightful point** in every meeting.

Phase 4: How to Get Promoted Without Asking for It

1. The "Ask for More Responsibility" Strategy

✔ Instead of **asking for a promotion,** ask for **bigger challenges.**

✔ Promotions follow responsibility—not the other way around.

💡 **Example:**

- **Mary Barra (CEO of General Motors) volunteered for high-stakes projects before getting promoted.**

◈ **Action Step:**

✔ Ask: *"How can I take on bigger challenges in my role?"*

2. Build Relationships with Decision-Makers

✔ Promotions **aren't just about performance—they're about influence.**

✔ People promote **those they trust and respect.**

💡 **Example:**

- **Networking within a company increases promotion chances by 70%.**

◈ **Action Step:**

✔ **Identify key leaders** and build relationships with them.

3. Create a Track Record of Leadership

✔ **Act like a leader before you become one.**

✔ Help others, take ownership, and lead projects.

💡 **Example:**

- **Tim Cook (CEO of Apple) was promoted because he acted like a leader years before getting the title.**

◈ **Action Step:**

✔ Start mentoring others and leading projects—even without the title.

Phase 5: Exercises to Fast-Track Your Promotion

1. The "What's My Value?" Audit

✔ Write down **three things** you do better than anyone else in your company.

✔ Focus on making these strengths **even stronger.**

💡 **Lesson: Your uniqueness is your greatest advantage.**

2. The "Executive Presence" Experiment

✔ Observe how senior leaders **speak, dress, and handle pressure.**

✔ Start **modeling these behaviors.**

💡 **Lesson: You get promoted when people already see you as leadership material.**

3. The "Visibility Boost" Challenge

✔ In the next **30 days**, find a way to:

- Speak up in a meeting.
- Take on a visible project.
- Share a success story with leadership.

💡 **Lesson: The more visible you are, the faster you rise.**

Conclusion: Promotions Go to the Stubborn, Not Just the Talented

✔ **Talent matters—but persistence matters more.**

✔ **If you make yourself indispensable, promotion becomes inevitable.**

✔ **Be so valuable that companies can't afford to lose you.**

💡 *"Don't wait for permission to be great—start acting like a leader now."*

🚀 **Next Chapter:** The Stubborn Work Ethic—How to Outlast and Outwork Everyone.

CHAPTER 24

The Stubborn Work Ethic—How to Outlast and Outwork Everyone

"There's no traffic on the extra mile."

— Grant Cardone

Introduction: Why Hard Work is Underrated

Most people want success, but few are willing to put in the **relentless effort** it takes to achieve it.

✔ **Talent can give you an edge—but work ethic determines who actually wins.**

✔ **Smart people quit when things get hard—stubborn people keep going.**

✔ **The most successful people aren't always the best—they're the ones who refuse to stop.**

💡 **This chapter will teach you how to develop an unstoppable work ethic—so that no one can outlast you.**

Phase 1: Why Most People Give Up Too Soon

1. The Myth of Overnight Success

✔ The world glorifies **fast success,** but the truth is:

- Most **"overnight successes" took 10+ years.**
- Behind every **big win is a stubborn refusal to quit.**

💡 **Example:**

- **J.K. Rowling was rejected by 12 publishers before Harry Potter became a billion-dollar brand.**

◈ **Lesson: Every success story starts with relentless persistence.**

2. Why Most People Don't Go All the Way

✔ **People quit when:**

- They don't see immediate results.
- It gets harder than expected.
- Others tell them to stop.

💡 **Example:**

- **Michael Jordan was cut from his high school team—but instead of quitting, he worked harder than ever.**

◈ **Lesson: Hard work beats talent when talent doesn't work hard.**

3. The "Comfort Trap" That Kills Success

✔ Most people choose **comfort over effort.**

✔ They stop when things feel "good enough."

💡 **Example:**

- **Tom Brady wasn't the most talented QB—but his extreme discipline kept him playing at an elite level into his 40s.**

◈ **Lesson: Being stubborn about growth keeps you ahead.**

Phase 2: The 5 Rules of an Unstoppable Work Ethic

1. Show Up Every Single Day (No Matter What)

✔ Success is not about working when you feel like it.

✔ It's about **doing the work even when you don't want to.**

💡 **Example:**

- **Kobe Bryant would wake up at 4 AM to practice—because he knew talent wasn't enough.**

◈ **Action Step:**

✔ Set a **non-negotiable daily habit** related to your goal.

2. Be the First In, Last Out

✔ The most successful people **outwork everyone around them.**

✔ They go **beyond expectations—and that's why they win.**

💡 **Example:**

- **Howard Schultz (Starbucks) would wake up at 3:30 AM to build his business.**

◈ **Action Step:**

✔ Start your day **before others do—and stay longer when needed.**

3. Do the Boring Work That Others Avoid

✔ **Everyone wants success—but few want the tedious grind.**

✔ If you're willing to master the **boring basics, you'll dominate.**

💡 **Example:**

- **Warren Buffett reads 500+ pages a day—not because it's fun, but because it gives him an edge.**

◈ **Action Step:**

✔ Identify the **boring but crucial tasks** in your field—and master them.

4. Work Like No One is Watching

✔ Don't wait for motivation.

✔ Work as if **someone is always watching—because results don't lie.**

💡 **Example:**

- **Cristiano Ronaldo trains harder than his teammates—even when cameras aren't on him.**

◈ **Action Step:**

✔ Hold yourself to **higher standards than anyone expects.**

5. Use Failure as Fuel (Not as an Excuse to Quit)

✔ The best workers **use rejection and setbacks to fuel them.**

✔ They don't stop at failure—they push harder.

💡 **Example:**

- **Elon Musk's first three SpaceX rocket launches failed—most would have quit. He bet everything on a fourth attempt, and it worked.**

◈ **Lesson: Failure isn't the end—it's a test of persistence.**

Phase 3: Daily Habits to Develop Relentless Work Ethic

1. The "Two-Extra-Hours" Rule

✔ Success is often **just two extra hours of work per day.**

✔ Those extra hours separate **the great from the average.**

💡 **Example:**

- **Bill Gates worked insane hours in his early years—because he knew success required sacrifice.**

◈ **Action Step:**

✔ **Dedicate two extra hours daily to mastery.**

2. The "No Zero Days" Rule

✔ Never let a day go by without **doing something productive.**

✔ Even small progress compounds over time.

💡 **Example:**

- **Jerry Seinfeld writes jokes every day—no excuses. This built his career.**

◈ **Action Step:**

✔ Track your streak of **consecutive workdays** toward your goal.

3. The "Do One More" Mentality

✔ Push yourself beyond **what feels comfortable.**

✔ When you feel like stopping, **do one more.**

💡 **Example:**

- **David Goggins (ex-Navy SEAL) believes people quit at only 40% of their actual capacity.**

🔶 **Action Step:**

✔ The next time you want to stop, **do one extra set, one extra call, one extra hour.**

Phase 4: Outworking Everyone (Without Burning Out)

1. Work in Intense Sprints (Not Slow Drags)

✔ The best workers don't just work hard—they work smart.

✔ Short, **intense sprints of focus** beat long hours of distraction.

💡 **Example:**

- **Top CEOs use "deep work" sessions to maximize productivity.**

🔶 **Action Step:**

✔ Try **90-minute deep focus sessions** followed by breaks.

2. The "One-Day Reset" Strategy

✔ Stubborn effort doesn't mean **never resting.**

✔ Take **one planned rest day** per week to recharge.

💡 **Example:**

- **LeBron James takes recovery as seriously as training.**

◈ **Lesson: Smart recovery keeps you working harder for longer.**

3. Cut Out Low-Value Work

✔ Many people work hard, but on **the wrong things.**

✔ Focus only on **high-impact work.**

💡 **Example:**

- **Warren Buffett only focuses on "big moves" that generate massive impact.**

◈ **Action Step:**

✔ Identify **low-value tasks and eliminate them.**

Phase 5: Exercises to Build a Stubborn Work Ethic

1. The "Early Riser" Challenge

✔ Wake up **one hour earlier** than normal.

✔ Use that time for **focused, productive work.**

💡 **Lesson: Success starts before everyone else wakes up.**

2. The "Track Your Hours" Experiment

✔ For one week, **log every hour** you spend working.

✔ Identify **where time is wasted—and fix it.**

💡 **Lesson: Most people are only productive for a few hours per day—imagine if you optimized that.**

3. The "Impossible Task" Test

✔ Set a goal that **feels impossible.**

✔ Work toward it **with stubborn focus for 90 days.**

💡 **Lesson: Your limits are higher than you think.**

Conclusion: Work Harder, Work Smarter, Never Stop

✔ **Talent fades—work ethic doesn't.**

✔ **The person who refuses to quit will always beat the one who stops early.**

✔ **Outwork everyone, and success will have no choice but to find you.**

💡 *"The difference between ordinary and extraordinary is just a little extra."*

🚀 **Next Chapter:** How to Take Risks Without Fear—Using Stubbornness to Face the Unknown.

CHAPTER 25

How to Take Risks Without Fear—Using Stubbornness to Face the Unknown

"If you are not willing to risk the usual, you will have to settle for the ordinary."

— Jim Rohn

Introduction: Why Most People Fear Taking Risks

The biggest barrier to success isn't **lack of intelligence, talent, or resources**—it's **fear of risk.**

❌ **People play it safe because they fear:**

- Failing and looking foolish.
- Losing money, time, or opportunities.
- Leaving their comfort zones.

✔ But here's the truth: **Every breakthrough in history came from someone taking a massive risk.**

💡 **This chapter will teach you how to develop a stubborn, fearless mindset toward risk-taking—so you can seize bigger opportunities without hesitation.**

Phase 1: Why Risk is the Price of Success

1. The Hidden Cost of Playing It Safe

✔ **Most people think avoiding risk = security.**

✔ But in reality, playing it safe can be the **riskiest thing of all.**

💡 **Example:**

- **Kodak invented the first digital camera but ignored it—because they feared taking a risk. Now, they're irrelevant.**

💠 **Lesson: If you avoid risks, you risk missing out on massive success.**

2. Why Fear of Failure Holds You Back

✔ **Most people fear risk because they fear failure.**

✔ But failure is **not the opposite of success—it's part of the process.**

💡 **Example:**

- **Jeff Bezos took a massive risk starting Amazon—he even told investors it might fail. Today, it's worth over $1 trillion.**

💠 **Lesson: You don't have to eliminate fear—you just have to act despite it.**

3. The Difference Between Smart and Reckless Risk

✔ **Not all risks are good risks.**

✔ The key is knowing the difference:

- **Smart Risk:** A calculated decision with potential upside.
- **Reckless Risk:** A decision based purely on impulse.

💡 **Example:**

- **Elon Musk invested everything into Tesla and SpaceX—but it was a calculated move based on research and vision.**

◈ **Lesson: Don't fear all risks—fear the wrong ones.**

Phase 2: How to Take Risks Without Regret

1. Use the "What's the Worst That Can Happen?" Test

✔ Ask yourself:

- *"If I take this risk and fail, what's the worst possible outcome?"*
- *"Can I recover from it?"*

💡 **Example:**

- **Richard Branson only takes risks where failure wouldn't destroy him—this is how he built Virgin Group.**

◈ **Action Step:**

✔ If the worst outcome is something you can recover from—**the risk is worth taking.**

2. The "1% Risk" Rule

✔ Most people think taking risks means **huge, all-or-nothing decisions.**

✔ Instead, take **small, calculated risks** that push you forward.

💡 **Example:**

- **Before quitting his job, Tim Ferriss tested his business idea part-time—until it was safe to go all in.**

◈ **Action Step:**

✔ Start taking **1% more risk every week** to build your risk tolerance.

3. Learn to Love the Unknown

✔ **Uncertainty is uncomfortable—but it's where all growth happens.**

✔ Instead of fearing the unknown, **train yourself to embrace it.**

💡 **Example:**

- **People who succeed in startups, investments, and leadership thrive in uncertainty.**

◈ **Action Step:**

✔ Expose yourself to **uncertainty daily**—make bold decisions without overthinking.

Phase 3: The Stubborn Mindset of Risk-Takers

1. The "Fail Faster" Strategy

✔ The faster you fail, the faster you learn.

✔ **Every failure = data that helps you make better decisions.**

💡 **Example:**

- **Thomas Edison failed 1,000 times before inventing the light bulb—but every failure taught him something.**

◈ **Action Step:**

✔ Set a **goal to fail at something new every month—just to learn from it.**

2. The "10-Second Rule" to Stop Overthinking Risks

✔ If you hesitate too long, you'll **talk yourself out of a great opportunity.**

✔ The **10-Second Rule:**

- **When faced with a decision, give yourself 10 seconds to commit.**
- **If it aligns with your goals, do it—before fear talks you out of it.**

💡 **Example:**

- **Many people miss out on huge chances because they "think about it too long" and never act.**

◈ **Action Step:**

✔ Start using **the 10-second decision rule** in small situations first.

3. How to Build Risk Tolerance Like a Muscle

✔ The more **risks you take, the stronger your risk tolerance becomes.**

✔ **Think of risk-taking like lifting weights—it gets easier with practice.**

💡 **Example:**

- **Most successful entrepreneurs were once risk-averse—but they trained themselves to take bigger leaps.**

◈ **Action Step:**

✔ Start taking **one uncomfortable risk per day.**

Phase 4: How to Use Stubbornness to Push Through Fear

1. Train Yourself to Be Unshakable Under Pressure

✔ Fear will always exist—but **you can train your brain to ignore it.**

✔ **Expose yourself to uncomfortable situations** until fear loses its power.

💡 **Example:**

- **David Goggins (ex-Navy SEAL) constantly puts himself in extreme discomfort to grow mental toughness.**

◈ **Action Step:**

✔ Start **deliberately doing things that scare you.**

2. Surround Yourself with Bold Thinkers

✔ If you're surrounded by **risk-averse, fearful people**, you'll become like them.

✔ **Find people who push you to take action.**

💡 **Example:**

- **Most great entrepreneurs have a circle of high-risk, high-reward thinkers.**

◈ **Action Step:**

✔ **Audit your circle**—remove fearful people, add bold ones.

3. The "Nothing to Lose" Mindset

✔ The most fearless people think:

- *"What's the worst that can happen? I'll survive."*
- *"If I fail, I'll learn."*

💡 **Example:**

- **Muhammad Ali took massive risks in his career—but he always believed he had nothing to lose.**

◈ **Action Step:**

✔ Every time fear holds you back, **remind yourself: "I have nothing to lose and everything to gain."**

Phase 5: Exercises to Strengthen Your Risk-Taking Muscle

1. The "Daily Bold Decision" Challenge

✔ Every day, **make one decision that pushes you outside your comfort zone.**

💡 **Lesson: Risk-taking is a skill—practice it daily.**

2. The "Worst Case Scenario" Exercise

✔ Write down **the absolute worst outcome** of taking a big risk.

✔ Then write **how you would recover from it.**

💡 **Lesson: Most "worst-case" fears aren't as bad as you think.**

3. The "Say Yes to More" Experiment

✔ For one week, **say yes to every opportunity that scares you.**

💡 **Lesson: Most breakthroughs come from saying yes when you want to say no.**

Conclusion: Success is for the Bold, Not the Timid

✔ **Every great achievement came from someone who took a massive risk.**

✔ **Stubbornness helps you push through fear and embrace the unknown.**

✔ **You don't have to be fearless—you just have to act despite fear.**

💡 *"Fortune favors the bold."*

🚀 **Next Chapter:** The Stubborn Fitness Mindset—How to Stay Consistent in Your Health Goals.

CHAPTER 26

The Stubborn Fitness Mindset—How to Stay Consistent in Your Health Goals

> **"Discipline is choosing between what you want now and what you want most."**
>
> — Abraham Lincoln

Introduction: Why Most People Fail at Fitness

Millions of people start **fitness goals**, but very few stick with them.

❌ **They quit because:**

- Motivation fades.
- They don't see quick results.
- Life gets busy, and excuses pile up.

✔ But the people who succeed **aren't the most talented or genetically gifted—they're the most stubborn.**

💡 **This chapter will teach you how to use relentless stubbornness to stay consistent, no matter what.**

Phase 1: Why Most People Quit (And How to Overcome It)

1. The "All or Nothing" Trap

✔ Many people think **they have to be perfect** to succeed in fitness.

✔ But **perfection is a lie—consistency is what matters.**

💡 **Example:**

- **The most fit people don't work out perfectly every day—they just never fully stop.**

◈ **Lesson: Progress beats perfection.**

2. Why Motivation is a Lie

✔ **Waiting to "feel motivated" is why most people fail.**

✔ The truth? **Discipline beats motivation every time.**

💡 **Example:**

- **Jocko Willink (ex-Navy SEAL) wakes up at 4:30 AM to train—not because he feels like it, but because he's disciplined.**

◈ **Lesson: Do the work, whether you feel like it or not.**

3. The "Slow Progress" Excuse

✔ People quit because **they don't see results fast enough.**

✔ But **all great transformations take time.**

💡 **Example:**

- **Arnold Schwarzenegger took years to build his physique—he didn't expect results overnight.**

◈ **Lesson: Stay patient—small wins add up over time.**

Phase 2: How to Make Fitness a Stubborn Habit

1. The "No Zero Days" Rule

✔ Never let a day go by **without doing something for your fitness.**

✔ Even a **5-minute workout is better than nothing.**

💡 **Example:**

- **Dwayne "The Rock" Johnson trains daily—no excuses.**

◈ **Action Step:**

✔ Even on **lazy days, do at least one small workout.**

2. Train Like an Athlete (Even If You're Not One)

✔ **Athletes don't rely on motivation—they rely on routines.**

✔ Treat your fitness like a **non-negotiable part of your day.**

💡 **Example:**

- **Cristiano Ronaldo follows a strict training schedule, no matter what.**

◈ **Action Step:**

✔ Schedule workouts like **important meetings—and never cancel them.**

3. Make It Harder to Quit Than to Continue

✔ The easier it is to **skip workouts,** the more likely you'll quit.

✔ Set up your life so that **quitting is more painful than sticking with it.**

💡 **Example:**

- **Sign up for a competition or a fitness challenge—so quitting feels embarrassing.**

◈ **Action Step:**

✔ Make a public commitment to your fitness goal.

Phase 3: The Stubborn Nutrition Mindset

1. Stop Thinking of Food as "Good" or "Bad"

✔ Many people quit because **they feel guilty about eating "bad" foods.**

✔ The truth? **One bad meal won't ruin your progress—quitting will.**

💡 **Example:**

- **The best athletes eat for performance, not guilt.**

◈ **Lesson: Focus on long-term consistency, not short-term perfection.**

2. The "One Simple Rule" for Stubborn Eating

✔ **If you can't stick to a diet for life, it won't work.**

✔ The best nutrition plan is the one **you can stubbornly follow forever.**

💡 **Example:**

- **Diets fail because they are too extreme—focus on balance instead.**

◈ **Action Step:**

✔ Pick **one** small habit (e.g., drinking more water) and build from there.

3. The "Never Miss Twice" Rule

✔ If you eat something unhealthy, **don't make it two bad meals in a row.**

✔ One bad choice is normal—**two in a row becomes a habit.**

💡 **Example:**

- **If you overeat today, make sure your next meal is healthy.**

◈ **Lesson: Progress is about consistency, not perfection.**

Phase 4: How to Push Through Fitness Plateaus

1. When Progress Slows, Get Stubborn

✔ Most people quit when they **hit a plateau.**

✔ But plateaus are **normal—it's your body adapting.**

💡 **Example:**

- **Elite athletes adjust their training instead of giving up.**

◈ **Action Step:**

✔ Change **one thing** (increase weights, add intensity) to break a plateau.

2. The "More Weight or More Reps" Rule

✔ If you're not seeing progress, **increase one of two things:**

- **More weight** (heavier lifts).
- **More reps** (higher endurance).

💡 **Example:**

- **Powerlifters focus on adding weight, while runners increase endurance.**

◈ **Action Step:**

✔ Choose **one** to improve each week.

3. Track Progress Like a Scientist

✔ Most people quit because they **don't see how much progress they're actually making.**

✔ If you track progress, **you'll stay motivated.**

💡 **Example:**

- **Serena Williams tracks every workout and match to improve performance.**

◈ **Action Step:**

✔ Keep a **fitness journal** with your workouts, diet, and results.

Phase 5: Exercises to Strengthen Your Stubborn Fitness Mindset

1. The "Show Up Anyway" Challenge

✔ Train **on the days you feel like quitting.**

✔ Even a **short session** builds mental toughness.

💡 **Lesson: The best workouts happen when you didn't feel like doing them.**

2. The "90-Day Stubborn Fitness Commitment"

✔ Set a **90-day goal** (strength, weight loss, endurance).

✔ Track progress and **stay consistent no matter what.**

💡 **Lesson: Most people quit too soon—90 days creates momentum.**

3. The "Do It for the Future You" Test

✔ Every time you want to skip a workout, ask:

- *"Would my future self regret this?"*

💡 **Lesson: The pain of discipline is temporary—the pain of regret lasts forever.**

Conclusion: Fitness is About Who's Stubborn Enough to Keep Going

✔ **The strongest, fittest people aren't the most gifted—they're the most stubborn.**

✔ **You don't need motivation—you need discipline.**

✔ **If you refuse to quit, success is inevitable.**

💡 *"You don't have to be extreme, just consistent."*

🚀 **Next Chapter:** Overcoming Addiction and Bad Habits with Stubborn Determination.

CHAPTER 27

Overcoming Addiction and Bad Habits with Stubborn Determination

> **"First, you make your habits. Then, your habits make you."**
>
> — Jim Kwik

Introduction: Why Breaking Bad Habits Feels Impossible

Bad habits **steal your potential, drain your energy, and keep you stuck.**

✗ People stay addicted to unhealthy behaviors because:

- **They feel powerless to change.**
- **The habit has become automatic.**
- **Quitting feels harder than continuing.**

✔ But here's the truth: **The only way to break free is through relentless stubbornness.**

✔ **You have to be more stubborn than your bad habits.**

💡 **This chapter will teach you how to stubbornly break addictions and build habits that serve you instead of destroy you.**

Phase 1: Why Most People Fail to Quit Bad Habits

1. The Brain's Addiction to Comfort

✔ Your brain is **wired to seek pleasure and avoid discomfort.**

✔ Bad habits give you **short-term pleasure** but create **long-term pain.**

💡 **Example:**

- **Scrolling on social media feels good now, but wastes hours of your life.**

◈ **Lesson: Your brain doesn't care about success—it cares about comfort. You have to fight back.**

2. Why "Willpower" is a Weak Strategy

✔ **Willpower alone won't break a habit.**

✔ The real secret? **Stubborn structure and consistency.**

💡 **Example:**

- **Smokers who rely on "just willpower" fail 90% of the time.**
- **Smokers who create a structured quit plan succeed 50% more often.**

◈ **Lesson: If you don't create a system, the habit will win.**

3. The "One Last Time" Lie That Keeps You Stuck

✔ Most people fail because they **tell themselves they'll quit after "one last time."**

✔ This creates an endless cycle of delaying real change.

💡 **Example:**

- **Gambling addicts always believe their next bet will be the last—but it never is.**

◈ **Lesson: The only way to stop is to stop lying to yourself.**

Phase 2: How to Stubbornly Break Any Addiction

1. The "Identity Shift" Method

✔ Instead of trying to quit, **become the kind of person who doesn't do it.**

✔ Change your identity, and your habits will follow.

💡 **Example:**

- **Instead of saying, "I'm trying to quit smoking," say, "I'm not a smoker."**

◈ **Action Step:**

✔ **Rewrite your identity** based on who you want to be, not who you were.

2. The "Destroy Your Triggers" Strategy

✔ **Your environment controls your habits.**

✔ If you want to change, **eliminate the triggers that lead to bad habits.**

💡 **Example:**

- **If you're addicted to junk food, don't keep it in your house.**

◈ **Action Step:**

✔ Identify **your top three habit triggers** and remove them immediately.

3. The "Replacement Habit" Trick

✔ You can't just "stop" a habit—you need to **replace it with something better.**

✔ Otherwise, your brain will crave the old habit again.

💡 **Example:**

- **People who quit drinking and replace it with fitness succeed more often.**

◈ **Action Step:**

✔ **Find a positive habit** to replace every bad habit you eliminate.

Phase 3: The Stubborn Mindset for Breaking Free

1. The "90-Day No Compromise" Rule

✔ The hardest part of breaking a habit is **the first 90 days.**

✔ **If you survive 90 days without giving in, the habit will die.**

💡 **Example:**

- **Studies show that after 90 days, addiction cravings drop by 75%.**

◈ **Action Step:**

✔ **Commit to 90 days of zero compromise**—not even once.

2. The "Burn the Bridges" Strategy

✔ Most people fail because they **leave a way back to their bad habits.**

✔ **If you're serious, destroy your escape route.**

💡 **Example:**

- **If you want to quit drinking, tell everyone you know and remove all alcohol from your home.**

◈ **Action Step:**

✔ Remove **everything** that makes it easy to return to your old habits.

3. Use Stubbornness as a Weapon

✔ The only way to beat addiction is to **be more stubborn than the craving.**

✔ Make quitting a **personal mission—refuse to lose.**

💡 **Example:**

- **Athletes use their stubbornness to push through pain—you can do the same with habits.**

◈ **Action Step:**

✔ Whenever you feel tempted, say: *"I refuse to let this habit control me."*

Phase 4: How to Build Unbreakable New Habits

1. The "Atomic Habits" Rule

✔ Big changes don't happen overnight—they happen **one small step at a time.**

✔ **Focus on tiny daily improvements.**

💡 **Example:**

- **James Clear (author of Atomic Habits) suggests starting with just 2 minutes a day.**

◈ **Action Step:**

✔ Make your new habit **so small you can't fail.**

2. The "Don't Break the Chain" Method

✔ Success is about **showing up every day.**

✔ **Never miss two days in a row.**

💡 **Example:**

- **Jerry Seinfeld built his comedy career by writing jokes daily—never breaking the chain.**

◈ **Action Step:**

✔ Track your new habit **on a calendar—don't let yourself break the streak.**

3. The "Accountability or Punishment" Rule

✔ Make quitting **so painful** that you won't allow it.

✔ If you slip, **there should be real consequences.**

💡 **Example:**

- **People who put money on the line are 70% more likely to succeed in quitting habits.**

◈ **Action Step:**

✔ Make a public commitment—or set up a consequence for failure.

Phase 5: Exercises to Break Free from Any Bad Habit

1. The "One-Week Detox" Challenge

✔ Quit **one habit for just seven days**—and see how much better you feel.

💡 **Lesson: Short wins build long-term momentum.**

2. The "Reverse Habit" Experiment

✔ Instead of your bad habit, **replace it with the opposite action.**

✔ Example:

- **Instead of smoking when stressed, do 10 push-ups.**

💡 **Lesson: Train your brain to crave new habits.**

3. The "Write Your Future Self a Letter" Method

✔ Write a letter to yourself **about why you refuse to go back to your old habit.**

✔ Read it whenever temptation strikes.

💡 **Lesson: Your future self will thank you for today's stubbornness.**

Conclusion: You Are Not Your Bad Habits—You Are Your Decisions

✔ **Your past habits don't define you—your choices today do.**

✔ **Bad habits will only win if you let them.**

✔ **Be stubborn about becoming the best version of yourself.**

💡 *"Every next level of your life will demand a different version of you."*

🚀 **Next Chapter:** The Athlete's Stubbornness—Lessons from the World's Greatest Competitors.

CHAPTER 28

The Athlete's Stubbornness—Lessons from the World's Greatest Competitors

"Champions aren't made in the gym. Champions are made from something deep inside—a desire, a dream, and a stubborn vision."

— Muhammad Ali

Introduction: Why the Best Athletes Are the Most Stubborn

Athletes don't succeed because they're the most **talented**—they succeed because they're the most **stubborn.**

✔ They refuse to quit when others do.

✔ They push past pain and obstacles.

✔ They train when no one is watching.

💡 **This chapter will break down the stubborn mindset of elite athletes—and how you can apply it to your own life.**

Phase 1: The Stubborn Mindset of Champions

1. The Relentless Drive to Win

✔ **Average people stop when they're tired.**

✔ **Athletes keep going when their body screams at them to stop.**

💡 **Example:**

- **Michael Jordan practiced harder than anyone—even after winning championships.**

◈ **Lesson: Winners keep training when others celebrate.**

2. The "Prove Them Wrong" Fuel

✔ The best athletes use **doubt as motivation.**

✔ If someone tells them they can't do it, they **stubbornly prove them wrong.**

💡 **Example:**

- **Cristiano Ronaldo was told he was too skinny to play professionally—so he built himself into a powerhouse.**

◈ **Lesson: Turn every doubt into fuel.**

3. The "Never Satisfied" Mentality

✔ Great athletes never think, *"I've made it."*

✔ They **constantly raise their own standards.**

💡 **Example:**

- **Serena Williams won 23 Grand Slam titles—but still trained harder than her competitors.**

◈ **Lesson: Success is never a finish line—it's just another starting point.**

Phase 2: Training Like a Champion (Even If You're Not an Athlete)

1. The "Outwork Everyone" Rule

✔ If you're not the most talented, **be the hardest worker.**

✔ **Effort beats talent when talent doesn't work hard.**

💡 **Example:**

- **Kobe Bryant was famous for practicing for hours before his teammates even arrived.**

◈ **Action Step:**

✔ Outwork **everyone in your field—make it impossible for them to keep up.**

2. The "No Excuses" Mindset

✔ Athletes train **even when they don't feel like it.**

✔ **They don't let bad days stop them—they push through.**

💡 **Example:**

- **Tom Brady won a Super Bowl at 43 years old—because he never allowed excuses.**

◈ **Lesson: Don't wait for the perfect moment—just show up and do the work.**

3. The "Train Through Pain" Mentality

✔ Athletes **embrace discomfort—they don't run from it.**

✔ **They know pain is temporary, but victory lasts forever.**

💡 **Example:**

- **David Goggins ran 100 miles on broken feet—because his mind was stronger than his body.**

◈ **Action Step:**

✔ The next time you feel **like quitting, push 10% harder instead.**

Phase 3: How to Handle Pressure Like an Elite Competitor

1. The "Big Game" Mentality

✔ Champions **thrive under pressure.**

✔ Instead of fearing big moments, **they embrace them.**

💡 **Example:**

- **Usain Bolt didn't get nervous before races—he saw them as opportunities to dominate.**

◈ **Lesson: When the stakes are high, don't shrink—rise.**

2. The "Short-Term Memory" Trick

✔ Athletes **fail all the time**—but they never dwell on mistakes.

✔ **They move on instantly and focus on the next play.**

💡 **Example:**

- **LeBron James forgets missed shots instantly—so he never loses confidence.**

◈ **Action Step:**

✔ When you make a mistake, **reset immediately—don't let it slow you down.**

3. The "Pressure Makes You Better" Belief

✔ **Pressure is a privilege.**

✔ **If you feel pressure, it means you're doing something important.**

💡 **Example:**

- **Simone Biles embraces Olympic pressure—because she knows only the best get to feel it.**

◈ **Lesson: Instead of fearing pressure, welcome it—it means you're leveling up.**

Phase 4: How to Stay Stubborn When No One Believes in You

1. The "No One Can Stop Me" Mindset

✔ Champions don't wait for **permission to succeed.**

✔ They believe, **"I will win—no matter what."**

💡 **Example:**

- **Conor McGregor told the world he would be a champion—before anyone believed in him.**

◈ **Action Step:**

✔ Tell yourself **every single day: "I am unstoppable."**

2. The "Alone in the Gym" Mentality

✔ The real work happens **when no one is watching.**

✔ Champions train in **silence—so they can shine when it matters.**

💡 **Example:**

- **Floyd Mayweather would train at 3 AM while his opponents slept.**

◈ **Lesson: Your competition might stop—make sure you don't.**

3. The "Stay Hungry" Rule

✔ **Most people slow down after a little success.**

✔ But champions **stay hungry—even after winning.**

💡 **Example:**

- **Michael Phelps trained for 6 hours a day—even after winning 23 gold medals.**

◈ **Lesson: Never let success make you comfortable.**

Phase 5: Exercises to Build an Athlete's Stubborn Mindset

1. The "Train When You Don't Want To" Challenge

✔ Show up **even when you don't feel like it.**

✔ These are the days that separate winners from quitters.

💡 **Lesson: Discipline = doing the work no matter what.**

2. The "Prove Them Wrong" Exercise

✔ Write down **every time someone doubted you.**

✔ Use that as fuel to **push harder than ever.**

💡 **Lesson: Turn doubt into motivation.**

3. The "Be the First One In" Experiment

✔ Show up earlier than anyone else.

✔ Be the hardest worker in the room—**and let your results speak.**

💡 **Lesson: If you work harder, you will always be ahead.**

Conclusion: Stubbornness Separates Champions from Everyone Else

✔ **The greatest athletes aren't the most talented—they're the most stubborn.**

✔ **They refuse to quit. They refuse to back down.**

✔ **You don't have to be an athlete to think like one—you just have to be willing to push past your limits.**

💡 *"You don't have to be the best. You just have to be the last one standing."*

🚀 **Next Chapter:** Mastering Self-Discipline—The Power of Stubborn Routines.

CHAPTER 29

Mastering Self-Discipline—The Power of Stubborn Routines

"You will never always be motivated. You have to learn to be disciplined."

— Unknown

Introduction: Why Self-Discipline is the Ultimate Superpower

Most people believe success comes from:

❌ **Luck**

❌ **Talent**

❌ **Motivation**

✔ But the truth? **Success is about discipline.**

✔ **Stubborn routines create unstoppable results.**

💡 **This chapter will teach you how to develop ironclad discipline—so that success becomes automatic.**

Phase 1: Why Most People Fail at Discipline

1. The "Motivation Myth"

✔ Most people fail because they **rely on motivation.**

✔ But motivation is **temporary—discipline is permanent.**

💡 **Example:**

- **Jocko Willink (ex-Navy SEAL) says he NEVER relies on motivation—only routine.**

◈ **Lesson: Discipline is doing the work, even when you don't feel like it.**

2. The "Excuse Loop" That Keeps People Stuck

✔ People tell themselves:

- *"I'll start tomorrow."*
- *"I'm too busy today."*
- *"I don't feel like it."*

✔ These **small excuses** create a **lifetime of regret.**

💡 **Example:**

- **Kobe Bryant worked out at 4 AM daily—because discipline doesn't wait for the "right time."**

◈ **Lesson: You can make excuses or progress—not both.**

3. The Science Behind Why Habits Stick

✔ Your brain **loves patterns.**

✔ The more you repeat an action, **the easier it becomes.**

💡 **Example:**

- **After 66 days, habits become automatic—no willpower needed.**

🔷 **Lesson: Discipline isn't about being strong—it's about repeating the same small actions daily.**

Phase 2: How to Build Unbreakable Self-Discipline

1. The "Make It Non-Negotiable" Rule

✔ Treat your habits like **breathing—you don't "decide" to breathe, you just do it.**

✔ Success must become a **requirement, not an option.**

💡 **Example:**

- **Dwayne "The Rock" Johnson trains daily—not because he feels like it, but because it's his standard.**

🔷 **Action Step:**

✔ Pick **one** habit and commit to doing it **daily—no excuses.**

2. The "5-Minute Rule" to Overcome Laziness

✔ **The hardest part is starting.**

✔ If you feel lazy, **tell yourself you'll do just 5 minutes.**

✔ 99% of the time, **you'll keep going.**

💡 **Example:**

- **Writers like Stephen King force themselves to write just one sentence—then momentum takes over.**

◈ **Action Step:**

✔ Next time you feel stuck, **commit to just 5 minutes.**

3. The "Stack Your Habits" Trick

✔ Attach new habits **to things you already do.**

✔ This **tricks your brain** into making them automatic.

💡 **Example:**

- **If you drink coffee daily, add 10 push-ups right after.**

◈ **Action Step:**

✔ Pair a new habit **with an existing one.**

Phase 3: How to Stay Disciplined (Even When Life Gets Hard)

1. The "Discipline Over Feelings" Rule

✔ Stop asking yourself:

- *"Do I feel like it?"*

✔ Instead, ask:

- *"Is this my standard?"*

💡 **Example:**

- **Serena Williams doesn't train based on her mood—she trains based on her mission.**

◈ **Lesson: Don't let feelings decide your actions.**

2. The "Never Miss Twice" Rule

✔ Missing **one day won't ruin you—but missing two builds failure.**

✔ If you slip up, **immediately reset the next day.**

💡 **Example:**

- **Top performers don't aim for perfection—they aim for consistency.**

◈ **Action Step:**

✔ If you miss a habit, **restart it the next day—no exceptions.**

3. The "System Over Willpower" Strategy

✔ Willpower is **limited—but systems last forever.**

✔ **Set up your life** so that discipline happens automatically.

💡 **Example:**

- **Athletes have set training times—so they never "choose" when to train.**

◈ **Action Step:**

✔ Create **a schedule where success is built into your day.**

Phase 4: How to Make Discipline a Lifelong Habit

1. The "Identity Shift" Trick

✔ **Don't just "try" to be disciplined—become the kind of person who is.**

✔ **Identity drives behavior.**

💡 **Example:**

- **Instead of saying, "I'm trying to be fit," say, "I am an athlete."**

◈ **Action Step:**

✔ **Rewrite your identity statement today.**

2. The "Pain vs. Pleasure" Motivation Hack

✔ People avoid pain more than they seek pleasure.

✔ If you link **pain to skipping discipline,** you'll never quit.

💡 **Example:**

- **Arnold Schwarzenegger visualized losing before every workout—so he never skipped training.**

◈ **Action Step:**

✔ Imagine **the pain of staying the same—use it to fuel your discipline.**

3. The "Accountability or Punishment" Strategy

✔ Discipline **increases when there are real consequences.**

✔ Use **accountability to force yourself to follow through.**

💡 **Example:**

- **People who bet money on their goals succeed 70% more.**

◈ **Action Step:**

✔ **Make a bet with someone** that you'll stick to your habits.

Phase 5: Exercises to Strengthen Self-Discipline

1. The "Wake Up Early" Challenge

✔ Set your alarm **30 minutes earlier.**

✔ Train yourself to **win the first battle of the day.**

💡 **Lesson: Self-discipline starts the moment you wake up.**

2. The "Daily 1% Improvement" Experiment

✔ Improve **just 1% every day.**

✔ Over time, this leads to **massive transformation.**

💡 **Lesson: Small daily wins create unstoppable results.**

3. The "Do It When You Least Want To" Test

✔ Push yourself **on the hardest days.**

✔ This builds **mental strength that nothing can break.**

💡 **Lesson: The best time to be disciplined is when you don't feel like it.**

Conclusion: Discipline is the Difference Between Success and Regret

✔ **Success isn't magic—it's daily discipline.**

✔ **If you are stubbornly disciplined, success becomes automatic.**

✔ **Your habits today decide your future tomorrow.**

💡 *"Discipline is choosing what you want most over what you want now."*

🚀 **Next Chapter:** Using Stubbornness to Break Through Mental and Physical Limits.

CHAPTER 30

Using Stubbornness to Break Through Mental and Physical Limits

> **"When you think you are done, you are only at 40% of your true potential."**
>
> — David Goggins

Introduction: The Hidden Barrier Between You and Greatness

Most people think they know their **limits.**

❌ **They believe they can only work so hard, push so far, or endure so much.**

❌ **They quit when things get uncomfortable.**

✔ But the truth? **Your body and mind are capable of far more than you think.**

✔ **The difference between success and failure is how stubborn you are when things get hard.**

💡 **This chapter will teach you how to push beyond limits—so that nothing can stop you.**

Phase 1: Why Most People Give Up Too Soon

1. The "40% Rule" of Mental Strength

✔ Most people quit at **40% of their true capacity.**

✔ **Your brain lies to you** to keep you comfortable.

💡 **Example:**

- **David Goggins (ex-Navy SEAL) ran 100 miles in 24 hours—because he refused to listen to his mind's limits.**

◈ **Lesson: When your mind says "stop," you're only halfway done.**

2. The "Pain = Growth" Mindset Shift

✔ People avoid **pain, discomfort, and exhaustion.**

✔ But **pain is the gateway to growth.**

💡 **Example:**

- **Arnold Schwarzenegger said, "The last three reps are what make the muscle grow."**

◈ **Lesson: If it's painful, that means it's working.**

3. The Comfort Zone is the Enemy of Strength

✔ Your brain wants **comfort—but comfort kills progress.**

✔ If you always do what's easy, **you'll never get stronger.**

💡 **Example:**

- **Elite athletes train in uncomfortable conditions—so that nothing surprises them in competition.**

◈ **Lesson: The more discomfort you embrace, the stronger you become.**

Phase 2: How to Push Past Physical Limits

1. The "One More Rep" Rule

✔ When you feel like stopping, **do one more.**

✔ Over time, this **trains your mind to ignore fatigue.**

💡 **Example:**

- **Top bodybuilders don't stop at failure—they push beyond it.**

◈ **Action Step:**

✔ **Always add one extra rep, step, or mile.**

2. The "Breathe Through the Pain" Strategy

✔ When you feel like quitting, **slow your breathing.**

✔ This tricks your body into **feeling more in control.**

💡 **Example:**

- **Marathon runners use breath control to keep running past exhaustion.**

◈ **Action Step:**

✔ **When discomfort hits, control your breathing instead of panicking.**

3. The "Train in the Hardest Conditions" Method

✔ If you train in **tough environments, real challenges will feel easy.**

✔ Expose yourself to **extreme conditions to build resilience.**

💡 **Example:**

- **Floyd Mayweather trains in a heated gym—to make fights feel easy.**

◈ **Action Step:**

✔ **Make training harder than real performance.**

Phase 3: How to Push Past Mental Limits

1. The "Reframe the Pain" Mental Hack

✔ Instead of thinking **"this hurts,"** think **"this is making me stronger."**

✔ Your mind believes **whatever you tell it.**

💡 **Example:**

- **Navy SEALs chant "I love pain" to rewire their brains.**

◈ **Action Step:**

✔ **Turn struggle into fuel by changing your internal dialogue.**

2. The "Control the Voice in Your Head" Exercise

✔ Your inner voice can either **push you or hold you back.**

✔ Train yourself to **talk to yourself like a champion.**

💡 **Example:**

- **Muhammad Ali kept repeating, "I am the greatest"—and he became the greatest.**

◈ **Action Step:**

✔ **Replace self-doubt with words of power.**

3. The "Visualization Before the Battle" Trick

✔ Your brain can't tell the difference **between real and imagined success.**

✔ **If you visualize overcoming limits, you'll break them faster.**

💡 **Example:**

- **Michael Phelps mentally rehearsed every race before even stepping in the water.**

◈ **Action Step:**

✔ **Before a challenge, close your eyes and visualize victory.**

Phase 4: How to Make Limit-Pushing a Habit

1. The "Daily Discomfort" Challenge

✔ **Do one thing daily** that makes you uncomfortable.

✔ Over time, **you'll become mentally bulletproof.**

💡 **Example:**

- **Cold showers, early mornings, public speaking—every discomfort builds resilience.**

◈ **Action Step:**

✔ **Write down one hard thing to do daily—and do it.**

2. The "Hardest Task First" Rule

✔ Train yourself to **attack difficult tasks first.**

✔ This builds **mental dominance over procrastination.**

💡 **Example:**

- **Billionaires tackle their hardest challenge first thing in the morning.**

◈ **Action Step:**

✔ **Start your day with the toughest task.**

3. The "Surround Yourself with Tough People" Rule

✔ **You become as strong as the people around you.**

✔ If you surround yourself with **mentally weak people, you'll stay weak.**

💡 **Example:**

- **Elite athletes train with those stronger than them—to force their own growth.**

◈ **Action Step:**

✔ **Find people who challenge you and make you better.**

Phase 5: Exercises to Strengthen Your Stubborn Resilience

1. The "Go Until Failure" Challenge

✔ Pick any workout (push-ups, sprints, lifting) and **push until failure.**

✔ This builds **grit like nothing else.**

💡 **Lesson: When your body says stop, prove it wrong.**

2. The "One-Week Extreme Challenge"

✔ For one week, **do something that tests your limits daily.**

✔ Push beyond what you thought possible.

💡 **Lesson: Your mind and body can handle more than you realize.**

3. The "Silence the Weak Voice" Exercise

✔ Every time your brain says **"stop"** or **"I can't,"** respond with:

- *"I CAN."*
- *"WATCH ME."*

💡 **Lesson: Dominate your own thoughts—or they'll dominate you.**

Conclusion: You Are Capable of More Than You Know

✔ **Your limits are not real—they are self-imposed.**

✔ **Your body and mind can go further—you just have to be stubborn enough to push.**

✔ **Every time you break a limit, you prove to yourself that nothing is impossible.**

💡 *"The pain you feel today is the strength you'll have tomorrow."*

🚀 **Next Chapter:** Building a Legacy—How Stubborn People Change the World.

CHAPTER 31

Building a Legacy—How Stubborn People Change the World

"The people who are crazy enough to think they can change the world are the ones who do."

— Steve Jobs

Introduction: Why Most People Are Forgotten

Most people live their lives **without leaving a mark.**

❌ They follow the rules.

❌ They play it safe.

❌ They never push beyond what's expected.

✔ But the ones who **refuse to accept limits**? **They are the ones who build legacies.**

💡 **This chapter will teach you how to use relentless stubbornness to create something that outlives you.**

Phase 1: Why Most People Never Leave a Legacy

1. The Fear of Standing Out

✔ Society teaches people to **fit in.**

✔ But **you cannot make history by blending in.**

💡 **Example:**

- **Nikola Tesla was ridiculed for his ideas—but today, we use his inventions daily.**

◈ **Lesson: If you want to be remembered, don't be afraid to be different.**

2. The Comfort Trap

✔ People get comfortable with **small success** and stop pushing.

✔ **But legacies are built by those who refuse to settle.**

💡 **Example:**

- **Oprah Winfrey could have stopped after becoming a famous talk show host—but she built a media empire instead.**

◈ **Lesson: Good enough is the enemy of greatness.**

3. The "Waiting for Permission" Mistake

✔ **Most people wait for approval to take action.**

✔ **World-changers don't ask for permission—they create their own opportunities.**

💡 **Example:**

- **Elon Musk didn't wait for NASA's approval—he built SpaceX to revolutionize space travel.**

◈ **Lesson: If you want to change the world, stop waiting for permission.**

Phase 2: How to Build a Legacy That Lasts Forever

1. Think Bigger Than Yourself

✔ A true legacy **isn't about personal success—it's about impact.**

✔ Ask yourself: **How can I create something that lasts beyond me?**

💡 **Example:**

- **Mother Teresa didn't seek fame—she built a global movement of kindness.**

◈ **Action Step:**

✔ **Focus on impact, not just personal gain.**

2. Master the Art of Relentless Persistence

✔ The greatest legacies are built **by those who refuse to give up.**

✔ **Stubbornness is the key ingredient in all world-changing work.**

💡 **Example:**

- **Thomas Edison tested 10,000 times before inventing the lightbulb.**

◈ **Lesson: The difference between failure and legacy is persistence.**

---

3. Solve a Problem No One Else is Solving

✔ **All great legacies come from solving a problem.**

✔ Find a problem that **matters to you** and dedicate your life to fixing it.

💡 **Example:**

- **Bill Gates built Microsoft not to make money—but to put a computer in every home.**

◈ **Action Step:**

✔ **What problem can you solve that will change lives? Start there.**

Phase 3: How to Overcome Resistance and Keep Going

1. The "Ignore the Critics" Rule

✔ Every world-changer **faces resistance.**

✔ The difference? **They keep going anyway.**

💡 **Example:**

- **Walt Disney was fired for "lacking imagination." Today, his name is legendary.**

◈ **Lesson: If people doubt you, you're probably onto something big.**

2. The "Failure is Just Feedback" Mindset

✔ Most people fear failure—**but failure is a sign you're making progress.**

✔ **Every mistake teaches you something valuable.**

💡 **Example:**

- **Steve Jobs was fired from Apple—then came back and made it a trillion-dollar company.**

◈ **Lesson: Failure is only permanent if you quit.**

3. Surround Yourself with Other Visionaries

✔ **You become like the people you spend time with.**

✔ If you want to build a legacy, **be around people who think big.**

💡 **Example:**

- **The Wright brothers surrounded themselves with engineers, not doubters.**

◈ **Action Step:**

✔ **Find people who challenge you to think bigger.**

Phase 4: How to Make Your Work Outlive You

1. Document Everything

✔ If you want your ideas to last, **write them down, record them, or teach them.**

✔ **Ideas that are shared live forever.**

💡 **Example:**

- **Marcus Aurelius' journal (Meditations) is still inspiring people 2,000 years later.**

◈ **Action Step:**

✔ **Start documenting your ideas and work.**

2. Build Something Bigger Than Yourself

✔ Legacies aren't about personal fame—they're about **creating something timeless.**

💡 **Example:**

- **Henry Ford didn't just build cars—he built an industry.**

◈ **Lesson: Create something that continues even after you're gone.**

3. Pass It On to the Next Generation

✔ True success isn't just **what you accomplish—it's what you teach others.**

💡 **Example:**

- **Nelson Mandela's work didn't end when he left—he created a movement that lasted.**

◈ **Action Step:**

✔ **Who will carry on your work? Teach them now.**

Phase 5: Exercises to Start Building Your Legacy Today

1. The "What Will They Say?" Reflection

✔ Imagine your funeral. **What will people say about you?**

✔ If you don't like the answer, **change how you live today.**

💡 **Lesson: Live in a way that leaves something behind.**

2. The "One-Year Impact" Challenge

✔ If you had **only one year left to live**, what would you build?

✔ Start working on that **now.**

💡 **Lesson: A sense of urgency creates legendary work.**

3. The "Mentor Someone" Test

✔ Find someone younger **and teach them what you've learned.**

✔ **Your knowledge lives forever when you pass it on.**

💡 **Lesson: Legacy isn't just what you do—it's what you teach.**

Conclusion: You Were Born to Leave a Mark

✔ **Most people live and die unnoticed—but you don't have to.**

✔ **Your stubbornness can build something that lasts forever.**

✔ **The world doesn't remember those who played it safe—it remembers those who refused to quit.**

💡 *"The goal is not to live forever—the goal is to create something that does."*

🚀 **Next Chapter:** The Stubborn Parent—Raising Strong, Resilient, and Independent Kids.

CHAPTER 32

The Stubborn Parent—Raising Strong, Resilient, and Independent Kids

> **"Don't prepare the road for the child. Prepare the child for the road."**
>
> — Unknown

Introduction: Why Parenting Requires Stubbornness

Parenting is **one of the hardest jobs in the world.**

❌ Society tells parents to **be soft, flexible, and accommodating.**

❌ But raising strong, resilient kids **requires stubborn discipline and firm values.**

✔ **If you are not stubborn about what matters, the world will shape your children for you.**

💡 **This chapter will teach you how to raise mentally tough, independent kids—by being a stubborn, intentional parent.**

Phase 1: Why Most Parents Get It Wrong

1. The Overprotection Trap

✔ Parents want to **protect their kids from struggle.**

✔ But **resilience comes from hardship, not comfort.**

💡 **Example:**

- **Children who experience small failures early in life develop stronger coping skills as adults.**

◈ **Lesson: Shielding your child from difficulty makes them weaker, not stronger.**

2. The "Everyone Gets a Trophy" Mistake

✔ The world now **rewards effort, even when results are poor.**

✔ But **real life doesn't work that way—there are winners and losers.**

💡 **Example:**

- **Michael Jordan was cut from his high school basketball team—if he had been "given a trophy" anyway, he may have never trained harder.**

◈ **Lesson: Let your child experience failure, so they learn to overcome it.**

3. The Fear of Saying "No"

✔ Many parents **want to be liked by their children.**

✔ But **kids don't need a best friend—they need a leader.**

💡 **Example:**

- **Strong, independent adults come from parents who enforced clear rules and boundaries.**

◈ **Lesson: If you say "yes" to everything, your child will struggle when the world says "no."**

Phase 2: The Stubborn Parent's Guide to Raising Resilient Kids

1. Teach Them to Solve Their Own Problems

✔ Don't **fix every problem for them—teach them how to fix it themselves.**

💡 **Example:**

- **Instead of rushing in to help when they struggle with homework, let them struggle first.**

◈ **Action Step:**

✔ **Ask them questions instead of giving answers.**

2. Set High Standards (And Enforce Them)

✔ If you **expect more from your child, they will rise to meet those expectations.**

✔ **Challenge them to be better—not just "good enough."**

💡 **Example:**

- **Serena and Venus Williams' father set strict training schedules for them from childhood—because he believed in their greatness.**

◈ **Lesson: Expect excellence, and they will rise to it.**

3. Let Them Face Consequences

✔ **Natural consequences teach better than lectures.**

💡 **Example:**

- **If a child refuses to wear a jacket, let them feel cold. They will learn faster than if you argue.**

◈ **Action Step:**

✔ **Step back and let reality teach them lessons.**

Phase 3: Teaching Mental Toughness to Kids

1. Normalize Struggle

✔ Teach them: **Struggle is normal—not a reason to quit.**

💡 **Example:**

- **Great athletes like Kobe Bryant train through pain, because they learned struggle is part of growth.**

◈ **Action Step:**

✔ **Praise effort, not just results.**

2. Teach the "Harder, Not Easier" Rule

✔ When life gets hard, **don't encourage escape—encourage effort.**

💡 **Example:**

- **If they want to quit a sport because it's hard, challenge them to stay another season.**

◈ **Lesson: Make quitting the harder choice.**

3. Make Them Earn What They Want

✔ If you **give them everything, they will value nothing.**

💡 **Example:**

- **Teens who work for their own car respect it more than those given one.**

◈ **Action Step:**

✔ **Teach them to work for what they want.**

Phase 4: Raising Independent Thinkers (Not Followers)

1. Encourage Debate and Critical Thinking

✔ **Don't punish questions—reward them.**

✔ Teach them how to **challenge ideas with logic.**

💡 **Example:**

- **Steve Jobs built Apple by thinking differently—not by following blindly.**

◈ **Lesson: Independent thinking starts at home.**

2. Teach Them How to Handle Peer Pressure

✔ Most kids **follow the crowd because they fear rejection.**

✔ Teach them to **be stubborn about their values.**

💡 **Example:**

- **Teens who have a strong sense of identity are less likely to fall into bad influences.**

◈ **Action Step:**

✔ **Role-play peer pressure scenarios to prepare them.**

3. Teach Financial Independence Early

✔ Schools don't teach financial skills—**parents must.**

✔ **Entitled kids become broke adults.**

💡 **Example:**

- **Kids who learn to save and invest young become wealthier adults.**

◈ **Action Step:**

✔ **Give them a budget and let them manage their own money.**

Phase 5: Exercises to Raise a Stubborn, Strong Child

1. The "Do Hard Things" Challenge

✔ Give them a **hard task and let them struggle through it.**

💡 **Lesson: Resilience comes from discomfort.**

2. The "Own Your Mistakes" Rule

✔ Teach them to **take responsibility instead of blaming others.**

💡 **Lesson: Accountability creates strong character.**

3. The "Solve Your Own Problem" Experiment

✔ The next time they have a problem, **guide them instead of fixing it.**

💡 **Lesson: Problem-solving is a lifelong skill.**

Conclusion: Strong Parents Raise Strong Kids

✔ **If you want your child to be independent, you must be a strong leader.**

✔ **If you are stubborn about their values, they will be stubborn about success.**

✔ **The world doesn't reward weakness—raise a child who refuses to be weak.**

💡 *"Your job isn't to make their life easy. Your job is to make them strong enough to handle life."*

🚀 **Next Chapter:** The Stubborn Learner—How to Master Any Skill Through Relentless Improvement.

CHAPTER 33

The Stubborn Learner—How to Master Any Skill Through Relentless Improvement

> **"There are no limits. There are only plateaus, and you must not stay there—you must go beyond them."**
>
> — Bruce Lee

Introduction: Why Most People Never Master Anything

Most people **want** to be great at something—sports, business, music, public speaking, writing—but **few ever achieve mastery.**

❌ They quit when progress slows.

❌ They get distracted by new interests.

❌ They assume talent matters more than persistence.

✔ But the truth? **Mastery is about stubborn, relentless improvement.**

✔ **The best in the world aren't born talented—they refuse to stop improving.**

💡 **This chapter will teach you how to use stubbornness to master any skill—so you become unstoppable.**

Phase 1: Why Most People Struggle to Learn New Skills

1. The Myth of "Natural Talent"

✔ **Most people believe experts are "naturally gifted."**

✔ But **the best in the world became great through practice, not genetics.**

💡 **Example:**

- **Michael Jordan wasn't born a basketball legend—he was cut from his high school team and worked relentlessly to improve.**

◈ **Lesson: Mastery is a choice, not a birthright.**

2. The "Quick Results" Trap

✔ **People give up because they expect results too soon.**

✔ But **all great skills take time to develop.**

💡 **Example:**

- **J.K. Rowling spent five years writing Harry Potter before anyone cared.**

◈ **Lesson: Greatness is a slow build—not an overnight success.**

3. The Plateau Effect (Why Most Quit Right Before a Breakthrough)

✔ At first, learning is **exciting and easy.**

✔ Then **progress slows—and this is where most people quit.**

💡 **Example:**

- **Bruce Lee said most people stop when they plateau—but masters push through it.**

◈ **Lesson: If you push past the plateau, breakthroughs happen.**

Phase 2: The Stubborn Mindset for Mastery

1. The "Forever Student" Mentality

✔ **Never assume you "know enough."**

✔ **Masters stay curious, always looking for ways to improve.**

💡 **Example:**

- **Warren Buffett still spends 80% of his day reading—because he believes in constant learning.**

◈ **Action Step:**

✔ **Commit to lifelong learning—no matter how skilled you become.**

2. The "1000-Hour Rule"

✔ The key to mastery is **deep, intentional practice.**

✔ **The best don't just practice more—they practice smarter.**

💡 **Example:**

- **Chess grandmasters don't just play games—they analyze their losses to improve faster.**

◈ **Action Step:**

✔ **Dedicate structured time to improving, not just repeating.**

3. The "Failure is Data" Mindset

✔ Failure isn't the opposite of success—it's part of the path.

✔ **Every mistake teaches you what NOT to do.**

💡 **Example:**

- **Elon Musk says every failure in Tesla and SpaceX led to breakthroughs.**

◈ **Lesson: Instead of fearing failure, learn from it.**

Phase 3: How to Learn Any Skill Faster

1. The "10X Rule" for Practice

✔ If you want to be great, **practice 10X more than others.**

✔ **Most people do the bare minimum—masters do extra.**

💡 **Example:**

- **Kobe Bryant practiced at 4 AM while his competitors were still sleeping.**

◈ **Action Step:**

✔ **Increase your practice time—even if it's just 10% more.**

2. The "Break It Down" Learning Method

✔ Masters don't just practice—they **break skills into tiny pieces.**

💡 **Example:**

- **Instead of learning "guitar," master just one chord at a time.**

◈ **Action Step:**

✔ **Master small parts first—then put them together.**

3. The "Teach It to Someone Else" Trick

✔ The fastest way to master a skill? **Teach it to someone.**

✔ If you can explain it simply, **you truly understand it.**

💡 **Example:**

- **Richard Feynman (Nobel Prize winner) learned faster by teaching complex ideas in simple terms.**

◈ **Action Step:**

✔ **Find someone to explain your skill to—it will deepen your learning.**

Phase 4: How to Stay Stubborn When Learning Gets Hard

1. The "No Zero Days" Rule

✔ Never go a day without **practicing your skill—even for 5 minutes.**

💡 **Example:**

- **Top musicians practice daily—even when they don't feel like it.**

◈ **Lesson: A little progress every day adds up to massive success.**

2. The "No Plan B" Mentality

✔ Masters don't have backup plans.

✔ **They burn the boats—so success is the only option.**

💡 **Example:**

- **Arnold Schwarzenegger never planned for failure—he only saw success.**

◈ **Lesson: If you have a way to quit, you will. Remove it.**

3. The "Unshakable Confidence" Rule

✔ If you believe you **will succeed, you'll train harder.**

✔ **Doubt slows progress—conviction speeds it up.**

💡 **Example:**

- **Serena Williams believed she would be #1 long before she was.**

◈ **Lesson: Tell yourself daily: "I will master this."**

Phase 5: Exercises to Accelerate Learning and Mastery

1. The "90-Day Deep Focus" Challenge

✔ Pick a skill and **dedicate 90 days to focused improvement.**

💡 **Lesson: Massive improvement happens with extreme focus.**

2. The "Track Your Progress" Test

✔ Keep a **journal of your progress** to stay motivated.

💡 **Lesson: Seeing growth keeps you stubborn.**

3. The "Find a Mentor" Experiment

✔ **Learning from someone better than you speeds up success.**

💡 **Lesson: A mentor helps you avoid wasted effort.**

Conclusion: Mastery Belongs to the Stubborn

✔ **Anyone can become great—if they refuse to quit.**

✔ **Success isn't for the lucky—it's for the relentless.**

✔ **Be stubborn about learning, and nothing will be impossible.**

💡 *"If you want to be the best, be prepared to do what others won't."*

🚀 **Next Chapter:** How to Be Remembered—Using Stubbornness to Leave an Impact.

CHAPTER 34

How to Be Remembered—Using Stubbornness to Leave an Impact

"Legacy is not leaving something for people. It's leaving something in people."

— Peter Strople

Introduction: Why Most People Are Forgotten

Most people **live, work, and disappear**—never leaving a mark.

❌ They follow the crowd.

❌ They do what's expected.

❌ They never take a stand for anything.

✔ But the people who are **remembered forever?**

✔ They **refuse to be ordinary.**

💡 **This chapter will teach you how to use relentless stubbornness to build a legacy that lasts long after you're gone.**

Phase 1: Why Most People Don't Leave an Impact

1. The Fear of Standing Out

✔ Society tells people **to fit in.**

✔ But **no one remembers the ones who blend in.**

💡 **Example:**

- **Albert Einstein was considered "strange" and rejected by academics—until his stubbornness changed physics forever.**

◈ **Lesson: If you want to be remembered, stop trying to fit in.**

2. The "What Will People Think?" Trap

✔ Most people **play it safe** because they fear judgment.

✔ But **the greatest minds didn't care what others thought.**

💡 **Example:**

- **Oprah Winfrey was fired from TV because she was "unfit for news." She refused to quit—and changed television forever.**

◈ **Lesson: Ignore critics. They only matter if you let them.**

3. The "Someday" Excuse

✔ **Most people die with their dreams still inside them.**

✔ They **wait for the "right time" to make an impact.**

💡 **Example:**

- **Steve Jobs built Apple in his parents' garage—not when he was "ready," but when he was stubborn enough to start.**

◈ **Lesson: If you wait for the right time, you'll wait forever.**

Phase 2: How to Build a Legacy That Lasts Forever

1. Be Stubborn About Your Mission

✔ **Pick one thing you believe in—and never back down from it.**

✔ **Every world-changer had a stubborn obsession.**

💡 **Example:**

- **Nelson Mandela spent 27 years in prison—because he refused to give up on freedom.**

◈ **Action Step:**

✔ **What's your mission? Write it down and commit to it.**

2. Focus on Impact, Not Just Success

✔ **Chasing money or fame won't make you unforgettable.**

✔ **Helping others, solving problems, and creating change will.**

💡 **Example:**

- **Mahatma Gandhi led India to independence without seeking personal power.**

◈ **Lesson: The more lives you touch, the longer your legacy lasts.**

3. Do What Others Are Afraid to Do

✔ Most people **play it safe**—which is why **boldness is rare.**

✔ The ones who **dare to take risks are the ones who make history.**

💡 **Example:**

- **Elon Musk risked his entire fortune to build Tesla and SpaceX—because he was stubborn about his vision.**

◈ **Action Step:**

✔ **What's one bold move you've been afraid to make? Do it now.**

Phase 3: How to Overcome Resistance and Keep Going

1. The "Ignore the Doubters" Rule

✔ Every great leader was **laughed at before they were admired.**

💡 **Example:**

- **The Wright brothers were told flying was impossible—until they proved everyone wrong.**

◈ **Lesson: Doubt is a sign you're doing something worth remembering.**

2. The "Don't Be Afraid to Fail" Mentality

✔ Every failure **teaches you something.**

✔ **If you quit after failing, you'll never be remembered.**

💡 **Example:**

- **Walt Disney was rejected by 300+ investors before he built Disney.**

◈ **Lesson: Failure is just proof you're on the right path.**

3. Surround Yourself with Other Visionaries

✔ **Ordinary people discourage big dreams.**

✔ **Surround yourself with stubborn, driven people.**

💡 **Example:**

- **Steve Jobs built Apple with a small team of rebels—not rule-followers.**

◈ **Action Step:**

✔ **Find a group of people who challenge you to think bigger.**

Phase 4: How to Make Your Work Outlive You

1. Document Everything

✔ If you don't **record your ideas, they die with you.**

💡 **Example:**

- **Leonardo da Vinci's journals inspired inventions centuries later.**

◈ **Action Step:**

✔ **Write, record, or teach your ideas to the world.**

2. Teach Others What You Know

✔ The best way to create a lasting legacy? **Pass your knowledge to others.**

💡 **Example:**

- **Bruce Lee's teachings still inspire martial artists decades after his death.**

◈ **Action Step:**

✔ **Mentor someone who can carry your lessons forward.**

3. Solve a Problem That Matters

✔ **Every lasting legacy solves a problem.**

✔ Find a problem **bigger than yourself—and dedicate your life to fixing it.**

💡 **Example:**

- **Henry Ford didn't just build cars—he made transportation affordable for everyone.**

◈ **Lesson: If your work solves a problem, it will never be forgotten.**

Phase 5: Exercises to Start Leaving an Impact Today

1. The "What Will They Say?" Reflection

✔ Imagine your funeral. **What do you want people to say about you?**

✔ If you don't like the answer, **start changing how you live today.**

💡 **Lesson: Live in a way that makes people remember you for the right reasons.**

2. The "One-Year Impact" Challenge

✔ If you had **only one year left, what legacy would you build?**

✔ **Start working on that mission now.**

💡 **Lesson: A sense of urgency creates legendary work.**

3. The "Mentor Someone" Test

✔ Find someone younger **and teach them what you've learned.**

✔ **Your knowledge lives forever when you pass it on.**

💡 **Lesson: Legacy isn't just what you do—it's what you teach.**

Conclusion: The World Will Remember You for How You Lived

✔ **Most people are forgotten—but you don't have to be.**

✔ **If you are stubborn about your mission, your work will live beyond you.**

✔ **History is written by those who refuse to quit.**

💡 *"The goal isn't to live forever. The goal is to create something that does."*

🚀 **Next Chapter:** The Lifelong Stubborn Mindset—Turning Relentless Persistence into a Way of Life.

CHAPTER 35

The Stubborn Entrepreneur—How to Build a Business That Lasts

> **"Success is walking from failure to failure with no loss of enthusiasm."**
>
> — Winston Churchill

Introduction: Why Most Businesses Fail

Starting a business is **easy.**

Keeping a business alive? **That's where most people fail.**

❌ 80% of businesses fail in the first five years.

❌ Most people quit when they hit major obstacles.

❌ They lack the **stubbornness to push through the hard times.**

✔ But the entrepreneurs who succeed? **They refuse to give up.**

✔ **They pivot, adapt, and keep going no matter what.**

💡 **This chapter will teach you how to use stubbornness to build a business that survives, thrives, and lasts.**

Phase 1: Why Most Entrepreneurs Give Up Too Soon

1. The "Fast Success" Lie

✔ People expect **quick results—but business takes time.**

✔ The biggest mistake? **Quitting too soon.**

💡 **Example:**

- **Amazon didn't turn a profit for nearly a decade—yet Jeff Bezos kept going.**

◈ **Lesson: If you quit too soon, you never give your business a chance to grow.**

2. The Fear of Failure

✔ Most people **avoid risk** because they fear failure.

✔ But **failure is not the end—it's the beginning of success.**

💡 **Example:**

- **Henry Ford's first two businesses failed before he built Ford Motor Company.**

◈ **Lesson: Every failure teaches you something valuable—if you're stubborn enough to keep going.**

3. Listening to the Wrong People

✔ **Most people will tell you your idea won't work.**

✔ The difference between winners and losers? **Winners don't listen to doubters.**

💡 **Example:**

- **Howard Schultz was told his Starbucks idea would never work—today, it's a billion-dollar company.**

◈ **Lesson: If you believe in your business, don't let small minds talk you out of it.**

Phase 2: The Stubborn Entrepreneur's Mindset

1. The "Never Say Die" Mentality

✔ Business is **a game of survival.**

✔ If you're stubborn enough to outlast your competitors, **you win.**

💡 **Example:**

- **Elon Musk was nearly bankrupt in 2008 but refused to quit—now, he runs multiple billion-dollar companies.**

◈ **Lesson: The longer you survive, the more likely you are to succeed.**

2. The "Adapt, Don't Quit" Rule

✔ **Being stubborn doesn't mean being inflexible.**

✔ The key? **Stick to your vision, but be willing to adjust your strategy.**

💡 **Example:**

- **Netflix started as a DVD rental company—then pivoted to streaming and dominated the industry.**

◈ **Lesson: Be stubborn about success, but flexible in how you get there.**

3. The "Unstoppable Belief" Principle

✔ Every great entrepreneur had **a vision that others doubted.**

✔ **They succeeded because they believed when no one else did.**

💡 **Example:**

- **Walt Disney was rejected over 300 times before he secured funding for Disneyland.**

◈ **Lesson: If you don't believe in your business, why would anyone else?**

Phase 3: How to Handle Business Setbacks Like a Stubborn Entrepreneur

1. The "Money Will Run Out" Reality Check

✔ Every entrepreneur **faces financial struggles.**

✔ The question is: **Will you quit, or will you find a way?**

💡 **Example:**

- **Sara Blakely started Spanx with just $5,000—now it's a billion-dollar company.**

◈ **Lesson: Success isn't about how much money you start with—it's about how stubborn you are when money runs low.**

2. The "Customers Will Reject You" Rule

✔ Your first idea **might not be the one that works.**

✔ The key is to **keep adjusting until you find what people want.**

💡 **Example:**

- **Airbnb's founders were rejected 1,000+ times before people started using their platform.**

◈ **Lesson: Every rejection is feedback—use it to get better.**

3. The "Competitors Will Copy You" Challenge

✔ The moment you become successful, **others will try to steal your ideas.**

✔ Stubborn entrepreneurs **don't complain—they innovate faster.**

💡 **Example:**

- **Facebook crushed MySpace by adapting to mobile-first technology before its competitor.**

◈ **Lesson: Stay ahead by constantly improving your product or service.**

Phase 4: The Stubborn Entrepreneur's Success Formula

1. Solve a Problem No One Else is Solving

✔ Businesses that last **solve real problems.**

💡 **Example:**

- **Uber made transportation easier—now it's a global empire.**

◈ **Action Step:**

✔ **Ask yourself: What problem can I solve better than anyone else?**

2. Outwork Everyone

✔ You don't have to be **the smartest—you just have to be the most relentless.**

💡 **Example:**

- **Mark Cuban read every book on business before starting his company.**

◈ **Action Step:**

✔ **Commit to working harder than your competition.**

3. Build Something Bigger Than Yourself

✔ A lasting business **isn't just about making money—it's about impact.**

💡 **Example:**

- **Apple changed the way the world uses technology—it wasn't just about selling computers.**

◈ **Action Step:**

✔ **What's your long-term vision? Write it down and commit to it.**

Phase 5: Exercises to Strengthen Your Entrepreneurial Stubbornness

1. The "10 Rejections" Challenge

✔ Go out and **get rejected 10 times on purpose.**

✔ Learn to **handle rejection like a successful entrepreneur.**

💡 **Lesson: Rejection doesn't kill businesses—quitting does.**

2. The "No Days Off" Commitment

✔ Work on your business **every single day for 90 days.**

💡 **Lesson: Momentum builds when you show up daily.**

3. The "Find a Business Mentor" Task

✔ Learn from **someone who has built what you want to build.**

💡 **Lesson: The fastest way to success is to learn from those who've already made it.**

Conclusion: Stubborn Entrepreneurs Always Win

✔ **If you refuse to quit, you will eventually succeed.**

✔ **If you're willing to adapt, you'll always find a way.**

✔ **If you're stubborn about solving problems, your business will thrive.**

💡 *"Entrepreneurship is not about having the best idea—it's about refusing to quit."*

🚀 **Next Chapter:** The Stubborn Leader—How to Inspire and Command Respect.

CHAPTER 36

The Stubborn Leader—How to Inspire and Command Respect

> **"A leader is one who knows the way, goes the way, and shows the way."**
>
> — John C. Maxwell

Introduction: Why Most Leaders Fail

Leadership isn't just about **position or power**—it's about **stubbornly standing by your values and vision.**

❌ Most leaders fail because they want to **please everyone.**

❌ They **compromise their vision** when facing resistance.

❌ They try to be **liked** instead of being **respected.**

✔ But the world's greatest leaders? **They are stubborn about what matters.**

✔ **They inspire because they refuse to compromise on their principles.**

✔ **They lead with strength—not by asking for approval.**

💡 **This chapter will teach you how to use stubbornness to lead effectively, gain respect, and create lasting influence.**

Phase 1: Why Most Leaders Struggle to Command Respect

1. The "Trying to Be Liked" Mistake

✔ Many leaders **fail because they prioritize approval over results.**

✔ But **great leaders don't lead by popularity—they lead by conviction.**

💡 **Example:**

- **Abraham Lincoln made unpopular decisions—but they changed history.**

◈ **Lesson: If you try to please everyone, you will lead no one.**

2. The "Weak Vision" Problem

✔ A weak leader **doesn't know where they're going.**

✔ **People don't follow indecision—they follow confidence.**

💡 **Example:**

- **Steve Jobs had an unshakable vision for Apple—and he never let anyone dilute it.**

◈ **Lesson: A clear, stubborn vision makes you a leader worth following.**

3. The "Avoiding Conflict" Trap

✔ Many leaders **shy away from hard conversations.**

✔ But **true leadership requires making tough decisions.**

💡 **Example:**

- **Elon Musk fired underperformers at Tesla—because results mattered more than comfort.**

◈ **Lesson: Stubborn leaders don't avoid conflict—they face it head-on.**

Phase 2: The Stubborn Leader's Mindset

1. The "Lead by Example" Rule

✔ **People don't follow words—they follow actions.**

✔ If you want respect, **set the standard by how you operate.**

💡 **Example:**

- **General Patton didn't just give orders—he fought alongside his soldiers.**

◈ **Lesson: If you expect discipline, work ethic, and commitment—live it first.**

2. The "No Excuses" Mentality

✔ Weak leaders **blame circumstances.**

✔ Stubborn leaders **take full responsibility for everything.**

💡 **Example:**

- **Jocko Willink (Navy SEAL) teaches "Extreme Ownership"—great leaders own every outcome.**

◈ **Lesson: If you own your results, people will trust and respect you.**

3. The "Make Tough Decisions" Principle

✔ Leading means making hard choices—even when people resist.

✔ A strong leader isn't afraid to say "no."

💡 Example:

- Warren Buffett turned down millions in short-term deals—because he was stubborn about long-term success.

◈ Lesson: Weak leaders say yes to everything. Strong leaders say yes only to what matters.

Phase 3: How to Gain Instant Respect as a Leader

1. Be Unapologetically Clear About Expectations

✔ People respect leaders who know exactly what they want.

💡 Example:

- Jeff Bezos demanded customer obsession at Amazon—and never wavered from that vision.

◈ Action Step:

✔ Set high expectations and don't lower them for anyone.

2. Be the First to Do the Hardest Work

✔ Your team will only work as hard as you do.

💡 Example:

- Dwayne "The Rock" Johnson shows up at 4 AM to train—so no one can outwork him.

◈ Lesson: Outwork everyone, and they will respect you.

3. Stand Firm in the Face of Opposition

✔ **Every great leader is criticized.**

✔ **The weak break under pressure. The strong stand tall.**

💡 **Example:**

- **Margaret Thatcher was called "The Iron Lady" because she never backed down.**

◈ **Lesson: If you believe in something, stand firm—even when people push back.**

Phase 4: How to Inspire People to Follow You

1. Be Unshakable in Your Beliefs

✔ **People don't follow uncertainty—they follow conviction.**

✔ **If you believe in something, don't waver.**

💡 **Example:**

- **Martin Luther King Jr. refused to compromise on civil rights—his stubbornness changed history.**

◈ **Lesson: Conviction creates influence.**

2. Make Others Feel Like They Matter

✔ People follow leaders who **make them feel valued.**

✔ **Stubborn leadership isn't about ego—it's about inspiring others.**

💡 **Example:**

- **Richard Branson prioritizes his employees—so they give their best.**

◈ **Lesson: Show people you believe in them, and they will follow you anywhere.**

3. Give People a Mission Bigger Than Themselves

✔ **Great leaders don't just give orders—they inspire movements.**

✔ **People want to be part of something bigger than themselves.**

💡 **Example:**

- **John F. Kennedy made people believe in landing on the moon—NASA followed.**

◈ **Lesson: If you give people a great mission, they will work relentlessly for it.**

Phase 5: Exercises to Strengthen Your Leadership Stubbornness

1. The "Set a Standard" Challenge

✔ Pick **one** high standard and refuse to lower it.

💡 **Lesson: Stubborn leadership means setting a bar—and keeping it high.**

2. The "Make One Tough Decision" Test

✔ Choose a **hard decision you've been avoiding—and make it today.**

💡 **Lesson: Great leaders don't hesitate to make tough choices.**

3. The "Lead by Example" Rule

✔ **For one week, hold yourself to a standard higher than everyone else.**

💡 **Lesson: Respect is earned through action, not words.**

Conclusion: Stubborn Leaders Change the World

✔ **The best leaders aren't afraid to be firm.**

✔ **They stand by their values—even when it's unpopular.**

✔ **They lead with action, conviction, and relentless belief.**

💡 *"If your actions inspire others to dream more, learn more, do more, and become more—you are a leader."*

🚀 **Next Chapter:** The Stubborn Innovator—Turning Crazy Ideas into Reality.

CHAPTER 37

The Stubborn Innovator—Turning Crazy Ideas into Reality

"The ones who are crazy enough to think they can change the world are the ones who do."

— Steve Jobs

Introduction: Why Most Ideas Never Become Reality

The world is **full of great ideas**—but very few ever become reality.

❌ Most people **give up when they face resistance.**

❌ They **abandon ideas because no one believes in them.**

❌ They **wait for permission instead of creating the future themselves.**

✔ But true innovators? **They are stubborn.**

✔ **They believe in their vision—even when no one else does.**

✔ **They push forward—until the world catches up.**

💡 **This chapter will teach you how to stay stubborn about your ideas and turn them into game-changing innovations.**

Phase 1: Why Most People Give Up on Their Ideas

1. The "It's Too Risky" Excuse

✔ **Most people never start because they fear failure.**

✔ But **every big innovation looked crazy before it worked.**

💡 **Example:**

- **The Wright brothers were laughed at for believing humans could fly—until they proved it.**

🔹 **Lesson: If your idea feels risky, that's a sign it's worth pursuing.**

2. The "No One Believes in Me" Problem

✔ **Great ideas are often rejected before they succeed.**

✔ The key? **You must believe first—before anyone else does.**

💡 **Example:**

- **J.K. Rowling was rejected by 12 publishers before Harry Potter became a global phenomenon.**

🔹 **Lesson: If you need approval to continue, you'll never innovate.**

3. The "Waiting for the Perfect Time" Trap

✔ Most people **delay action because they want everything to be perfect.**

✔ But **there is never a perfect time—only now.**

💡 **Example:**

- **Elon Musk didn't wait for "perfect conditions" to build Tesla—he created them.**

🔹 **Lesson: Start before you're ready—figure things out along the way.**

Phase 2: The Stubborn Innovator's Mindset

1. The "See What Others Don't" Rule

✔ Most people only see the world as it is.

✔ Innovators see the world as it could be.

💡 Example:

- Steve Jobs envisioned a world where everyone had a personal computer—when no one else did.

◈ Lesson: If people don't see your vision yet, that's normal—keep going.

2. The "Fail Fast, Fail Forward" Mentality

✔ Failure isn't a roadblock—it's a stepping stone.

✔ The faster you fail, the faster you learn.

💡 Example:

- Thomas Edison failed 1,000+ times before inventing the lightbulb.

◈ Lesson: Each failure moves you closer to success.

3. The "Ignore the Experts" Principle

✔ Experts often say innovation is impossible—until someone proves them wrong.

💡 Example:

- Henry Ford was told "horses are the future"—he built cars anyway.

◈ Lesson: Trust your own vision, not the doubters.

Phase 3: How to Push Your Idea Through Resistance

1. The "Build Before You Ask for Permission" Rule

✔ Don't wait for validation—start building now.

💡 Example:

- Jeff Bezos didn't ask traditional retailers if Amazon was a good idea—he just built it.

◈ Lesson: If you wait for permission, you'll be waiting forever.

2. The "Prove Them Wrong" Strategy

✔ Let your results speak louder than criticism.

💡 Example:

- Netflix was mocked by Blockbuster—until it destroyed Blockbuster.

◈ Lesson: Focus on proving your idea works, not on defending it.

3. The "Stick to the Core Idea, Adapt the Execution" Strategy

✔ Be stubborn about your vision, but flexible about how you get there.

💡 Example:

- Instagram started as a check-in app—then pivoted to focus only on photos.

◈ Lesson: If something isn't working, adjust the method—not the mission.

Phase 4: How to Make Your Idea Unstoppable

1. Keep Improving Until People Can't Ignore It

✔ Your idea must be so good that people have no choice but to notice.

💡 Example:

- Airbnb started by renting out air mattresses—but improved until it became a billion-dollar company.

◈ Lesson: If people don't believe in your idea, improve it until they do.

2. Stay Obsessively Focused

✔ Don't chase distractions—go all in.

💡 Example:

- Bill Gates dropped out of Harvard to focus 100% on Microsoft.

◈ Lesson: Big success requires total commitment.

3. Surround Yourself with Believers, Not Doubters

✔ Find people who challenge and support your vision.

💡 Example:

- Elon Musk built a team of engineers who shared his belief in SpaceX.

◈ Lesson: A strong team makes your idea bulletproof.

Phase 5: Exercises to Strengthen Your Innovation Stubbornness

1. The "Ignore the Critics" Challenge

✔ Write down the **biggest doubts you've heard about your idea.**

✔ **Now, commit to proving them wrong.**

💡 **Lesson: Doubt is fuel—use it.**

2. The "Start Before You're Ready" Test

✔ Take **one step today** to push your idea forward.

✔ Even if it's small—**start now.**

💡 **Lesson: Action is more powerful than waiting for the "right time."**

3. The "Keep Going No Matter What" Rule

✔ Commit to **working on your idea daily for 90 days.**

✔ No skipping. No quitting. **Just progress.**

💡 **Lesson: Stubborn persistence turns ideas into reality.**

Conclusion: The Future Belongs to the Stubborn

✔ **The world doesn't reward those who quit—it rewards those who persist.**

✔ **Every breakthrough in history started as a crazy idea.**

✔ **If you refuse to give up, your idea will change the world.**

💡 *"The best way to predict the future is to create it."*

🚀 **Next Chapter:** The Stubborn Underdog—Winning When the Odds Are Against You.

CHAPTER 38

The Stubborn Underdog—Winning When the Odds Are Against You

> **"It's not the size of the dog in the fight, it's the size of the fight in the dog."**
>
> — Mark Twain

Introduction: Why the World Underestimates You

The world loves to **doubt underdogs.**

❌ People assume **if you start with less, you'll achieve less.**

❌ They say **you don't have the resources, connections, or background.**

❌ They **underestimate your hunger, your drive, and your stubbornness.**

✔ But underdogs have **one advantage: They are willing to fight harder.**

✔ **They use their disadvantages as fuel.**

✔ **They refuse to quit—no matter how bad the odds look.**

💡 **This chapter will teach you how to use stubbornness to turn disadvantages into strengths—and win when no one expects you to.**

Phase 1: Why Being the Underdog is an Advantage

1. The "Nothing to Lose" Power

✔ People with everything to lose play it safe.

✔ But underdogs take bigger risks—because they have nothing to lose.

💡 Example:

- Sylvester Stallone was broke when he refused to sell his Rocky script unless he played the lead role—now it's an iconic franchise.

◈ Lesson: When you have nothing to lose, you become fearless.

2. The "Hunger for Success" Advantage

✔ People who start with everything don't fight as hard.

✔ Underdogs are forced to work twice as hard to prove themselves.

💡 Example:

- Cristiano Ronaldo grew up in poverty—his hunger to escape made him one of the greatest footballers in history.

◈ Lesson: Your hunger is your secret weapon—use it.

3. The "No One Sees You Coming" Factor

✔ When no one expects you to win, you can surprise them.

✔ Being underestimated means people won't see you coming.

💡 **Example:**

- **Oprah Winfrey was told she wasn't fit for TV—now she's one of the most influential women in media.**

◈ **Lesson: Use their doubt as motivation.**

Phase 2: The Stubborn Underdog's Mindset

1. The "Prove Them Wrong" Mentality

✔ **The best revenge? Massive success.**

💡 **Example:**

- **Michael Jordan was cut from his high school basketball team—he used it as motivation to become the greatest of all time.**

◈ **Lesson: Turn rejection into fuel.**

2. The "No Excuses" Rule

✔ **Underdogs don't waste time complaining.**

✔ **They find a way to win—no matter what.**

💡 **Example:**

- **Helen Keller was deaf and blind—but still became a world-famous author and activist.**

◈ **Lesson: Your disadvantages are only excuses if you let them be.**

3. The "Use What You Have" Strategy

✔ **You don't need the best resources—you need the best mindset.**

💡 **Example:**

- **Dwayne "The Rock" Johnson started with $7 to his name—now he's a global icon.**

◈ **Lesson: Start where you are. Use what you have. Win anyway.**

Phase 3: How to Outsmart, Outwork, and Outlast Your Competition

1. Work Harder Than Everyone Else

✔ **Talent means nothing if you don't outwork people.**

💡 **Example:**

- **Kobe Bryant was the first to arrive at practice and the last to leave—every single day.**

◈ **Lesson: If they work 8 hours, you work 12.**

2. Turn Rejection into Resilience

✔ **Every "no" gets you closer to a "yes."**

💡 **Example:**

- **Walt Disney was rejected over 300 times before he secured funding for Disneyland.**

◈ **Lesson: Rejection is just proof that you're trying. Keep going.**

3. Never Let Anyone Set Your Limits

✔ **People will tell you what's "realistic"**—ignore them.

✔ **Only you decide what's possible.**

💡 **Example:**

- **Richard Branson dropped out of school and was told he'd never succeed—now he owns Virgin Airlines.**

◈ **Lesson: Dream big, then make it happen.**

Phase 4: How to Win When the Odds Are Against You

1. Keep Moving Forward—Even When It's Slow

✔ **Progress is progress—even if it's small.**

💡 **Example:**

- **J.K. Rowling wrote Harry Potter while struggling as a single mother—one page at a time.**

◈ **Lesson: Success is built through stubborn persistence.**

2. Use Every Setback as Fuel

✔ **Turn every failure into motivation.**

💡 **Example:**

- **Howard Schultz was rejected by 242 investors before Starbucks took off.**

◈ **Lesson: Every "no" brings you closer to a "yes."**

3. Stay Relentless Until You Break Through

✔ **The breakthrough always happens right after most people quit.**

💡 **Example:**

- **Colonel Sanders was rejected over 1,000 times before KFC became a success.**

◈ **Lesson: Keep going longer than everyone else, and you will win.**

Phase 5: Exercises to Strengthen Your Underdog Stubbornness

1. The "Who Doubts You?" Challenge

✔ Write down **the names of everyone who has doubted you.**

✔ **Keep this list as motivation to prove them wrong.**

💡 **Lesson: Doubt fuels the determined.**

2. The "10X Effort" Test

✔ Pick a goal—then **work 10 times harder than what's "normal."**

💡 **Lesson: Effort beats talent when talent doesn't work hard.**

3. The "Refuse to Quit" Commitment

✔ **For the next 6 months, commit to pushing forward—no matter what.**

✔ **No stopping. No excuses. Just progress.**

💡 **Lesson: Relentless effort always wins in the end.**

Conclusion: The Underdog Always Wins If They Refuse to Quit

✔ **No one expects you to succeed—use that as an advantage.**

✔ **Turn rejection into fuel, doubt into motivation, and obstacles into stepping stones.**

✔ **The world underestimates the stubborn. That's why they win.**

💡 *"Success is never owned. It's rented. And the rent is due every day."*

🚀 **Next Chapter:** The Stubborn Survivor—Overcoming Life's Hardest Challenges.

CHAPTER 39

The Stubborn Survivor—Overcoming Life's Hardest Challenges

> **"You never know how strong you are until being strong is your only choice."**
>
> — Bob Marley

Introduction: Why Some People Survive and Others Break

Life is **not fair.**

❌ Some people face **unimaginable hardship.**

❌ Others **fall apart at the first sign of struggle.**

❌ **Most people give up too soon—because they don't know their own strength.**

✔ But **the strongest people?** They are **stubborn survivors.**

✔ **They refuse to break, no matter what life throws at them.**

✔ **They don't just survive—they rise.**

💡 **This chapter will teach you how to be relentless in the face of life's hardest challenges.**

Phase 1: Why Some People Survive and Others Give Up

1. The "Why Me?" Mindset vs. The "Try Me" Mindset

✔ Weak people ask, **"Why is this happening to me?"**

✔ Survivors say, **"Try me—I'll find a way through this."**

💡 **Example:**

- **Viktor Frankl survived the Holocaust because he refused to let suffering define him.**

◈ **Lesson: Your mindset determines whether you break or rise.**

2. The "Waiting to Be Rescued" Mistake

✔ **Most people wait for help—but help doesn't always come.**

✔ **Survivors take control, even in the worst situations.**

💡 **Example:**

- **Bethany Hamilton lost her arm in a shark attack—yet she kept surfing and became a world champion.**

◈ **Lesson: Don't wait for a savior—be your own.**

3. The "Pain = Weakness" Lie

✔ **Most people think pain is a reason to stop.**

✔ **Survivors know pain is proof of growth.**

💡 **Example:**

- **Malala Yousafzai was shot for fighting for education—she didn't stop, she got stronger.**

◈ **Lesson: Pain isn't an enemy—it's part of the process.**

Phase 2: The Stubborn Survivor's Mindset

1. The "No Matter What" Mentality

✔ Survivors make **one decision: No matter what, I keep going.**

💡 **Example:**

- **Nelson Mandela spent 27 years in prison—but never gave up on his mission.**

◈ **Lesson: If you refuse to stop, you will outlast any hardship.**

2. The "Adapt, Don't Break" Rule

✔ **Survivors don't give up—they adjust.**

✔ **They find another way when the path is blocked.**

💡 **Example:**

- **Stephen Hawking was diagnosed with ALS and lost mobility—but became one of history's greatest scientists.**

◈ **Lesson: If one door closes, find another way in.**

3. The "Strength Comes from Struggle" Principle

✔ **Survivors use pain as fuel, not as an excuse.**

💡 **Example:**

- **Oprah Winfrey was abused as a child—yet she built an empire from nothing.**

◈ **Lesson: Your hardest moments can make you unstoppable—if you let them.**

Phase 3: How to Push Through the Worst Moments in Life

1. Take Control of What You Can

✔ **You can't control everything—but you can always control something.**

💡 **Example:**

- **J.K. Rowling wrote Harry Potter while struggling as a single mother—one page at a time.**

◈ **Lesson: Find one thing you CAN do, and do it every day.**

2. Refuse to Stay Down

✔ **Everyone gets knocked down—survivors get back up.**

💡 **Example:**

- **Thomas Edison's lab burned down—but he rebuilt and kept inventing.**

◈ **Lesson: Losing everything doesn't mean you've lost—unless you quit.**

3. Find Meaning in the Struggle

✔ **Survivors turn pain into purpose.**

💡 **Example:**

- **Nick Vujicic was born without arms or legs—he now inspires millions worldwide.**

◈ **Lesson: If you give your struggle a purpose, it can fuel you.**

Phase 4: How to Build Unbreakable Resilience

1. Toughen Your Mind Every Day

✔ **Strength is built through small struggles.**

💡 **Example:**

- **David Goggins ran 100 miles in 24 hours—because he trained his mind, not just his body.**

◈ **Lesson: Train yourself to handle discomfort daily.**

2. Build a "Never Quit" System

✔ **Survivors create routines that force them to keep going.**

💡 **Example:**

- **Tony Robbins jumps into freezing water every morning—to train his mind for discomfort.**

◈ **Lesson: Create daily habits that make you mentally stronger.**

3. Surround Yourself with Fighters, Not Quitters

✔ **Your environment shapes you—choose wisely.**

💡 **Example:**

- **Athletes train with champions—not with complainers.**

◈ **Lesson: Find people who push you forward, not pull you down.**

Phase 5: Exercises to Strengthen Your Survivor Stubbornness

1. The "No Complaining" Challenge

✔ Go **one week without complaining.**

✔ Instead, **find solutions.**

💡 **Lesson: Complaining weakens you—action strengthens you.**

2. The "Do Something Hard Every Day" Test

✔ **Every day, do something uncomfortable.**

💡 **Lesson: Discomfort makes you stronger.**

3. The "Write Your Comeback Story" Exercise

✔ Write a **letter to your future self—describing how you overcame this struggle.**

💡 **Lesson: If you can imagine your comeback, you can create it.**

Conclusion: Survivors Always Win in the End

✔ **Life will test you—but you don't have to break.**

✔ **Every challenge can make you stronger—if you refuse to quit.**

✔ **You are not weak. You are stubborn. And that makes you unbreakable.**

💡 *"Hard times create strong people. Be one of them."*

🚀 **Next Chapter:** The Stubborn Entrepreneur—Building a Business That Lasts.

CHAPTER 40

The Lifelong Stubborn Mindset—Turning Relentless Persistence into a Way of Life

> **"A river cuts through rock, not because of its power, but because of its persistence."**
>
> — James N. Watkins

Introduction: Why Most People Lose Their Stubbornness Over Time

At some point, **most people give up.**

❌ They start strong but lose motivation.

❌ They face setbacks and assume they'll never succeed.

❌ They let life wear them down instead of pushing back.

✔ But the people who **achieve the impossible?**

✔ **They don't just use stubbornness for a short time—they live it.**

✔ **They turn persistence into a way of life.**

💡 **This chapter will teach you how to make relentless stubbornness your default mindset—for success in every area of life.**

Phase 1: Why Most People Give Up Too Soon

1. They Let Failure Define Them

✔ Most people **take failure personally.**

✔ **Instead of learning, they quit.**

💡 **Example:**

- **Colonel Sanders' fried chicken recipe was rejected 1,000+ times—but he refused to quit.**

◈ **Lesson: Failure is never final—unless you let it be.**

2. They Get Comfortable

✔ **Comfort kills ambition.**

✔ **The moment you stop pushing, you stop growing.**

💡 **Example:**

- **Muhammad Ali kept training even after becoming a champion—because he knew success is never permanent.**

◈ **Lesson: The moment you relax, you start losing.**

3. They Stop Reinventing Themselves

✔ **If you don't grow, you get left behind.**

💡 **Example:**

- **Blockbuster refused to adapt—Netflix crushed them.**

◈ **Lesson: Winners stay stubborn about growth, not just past success.**

Phase 2: The Lifelong Stubborn Mindset

1. Never Accept a "Final" Defeat

✔ If something isn't working, find another way.

💡 Example:

- Einstein failed as a student—but changed physics forever.

◈ Lesson: There's always another path—keep looking.

2. Stay Hungry, No Matter How Much You Succeed

✔ True winners never lose their hunger.

💡 Example:

- Michael Jordan won 6 championships—but kept training as if he had never won.

◈ Lesson: The best never stop improving.

3. Stay in the Game Longer Than Anyone Else

✔ The longer you play, the higher your chances of winning.

💡 Example:

- Warren Buffett has been investing for 70+ years—his patience built his empire.

◈ Lesson: Stubborn longevity beats short-term effort.

Phase 3: How to Stay Stubborn for Life—Without Burning Out

1. Find a Mission Bigger Than Yourself

✔ The strongest stubbornness comes from purpose.

💡 **Example:**

- **Mother Teresa didn't work for money—she worked for humanity.**

◈ **Lesson: When your mission is bigger than you, quitting isn't an option.**

2. Create Routines That Force You to Stay Relentless

✔ **Habits create consistency—even when motivation fades.**

💡 **Example:**

- **Jocko Willink wakes up at 4:30 AM every day—discipline makes him unstoppable.**

◈ **Lesson: Your habits must be stronger than your emotions.**

3. Surround Yourself with Unstoppable People

✔ **You become who you spend time with.**

💡 **Example:**

- **Serena Williams trained with the best—because champions sharpen champions.**

◈ **Lesson: Find people who refuse to quit, just like you.**

Phase 4: The Ultimate Stubbornness Test—Can You Stick with It for 10 Years?

1. Most People Quit in Months—Will You Last a Decade?

✔ **Every big success story took years—not months.**

💡 **Example:**

- **Jeff Bezos worked on Amazon for years before it made a profit.**

◈ **Lesson: Can you stay focused for 10 years? That's how real success happens.**

2. Track Your Progress Over Time

✔ **Small progress adds up to massive success.**

💡 **Example:**

- **Writing 1 page a day = 365 pages (a book) in a year.**

◈ **Lesson: Consistency beats bursts of effort.**

3. Build a Legacy, Not Just a Life

✔ **Work on something that will outlive you.**

💡 **Example:**

- **Steve Jobs didn't just build Apple—he built a culture of innovation.**

◈ **Lesson: Make an impact that lasts beyond you.**

Phase 5: Exercises to Make Stubbornness a Lifelong Habit

1. The "No Matter What" Commitment

✔ Pick **one** goal.

✔ Commit to it for **10 years—no excuses.**

💡 **Lesson: Mastery requires long-term commitment.**

2. The "Unstoppable Habit" Test

✔ Choose **one habit** that will make you stronger.

✔ Do it **every day for a year.**

💡 **Lesson: Greatness is built on small, stubborn actions.**

3. The "Rewrite Your Story" Exercise

✔ Write down your biggest failures.

✔ **Now, rewrite them as stepping stones to success.**

💡 **Lesson: Your story isn't over yet—turn failures into fuel.**

Conclusion: Be the Person Who Never Quits

✔ **The world belongs to those who refuse to give up.**

✔ **You can be that person—if you make stubbornness a way of life.**

✔ **Most people quit. Don't be most people.**

💡 *"The best don't quit. The best keep going—even when no one believes in them."*

🚀 **Final Words: Your Stubborn Journey Starts Now.**

www.ingramcontent.com/pod-product-compliance
Lightning Source LLC
Chambersburg PA
CBHW032006150726
47990CB00005B/1852
* 9 7 9 8 8 9 7 2 4 5 5 6 7 *